D1499195

When You Don't Know
WHAT TO PRAY

When You Don't Know
WHAT TO PRAY

100 ESSENTIAL PRAYERS
FOR ENDURING LIFE'S STORMS

CHARLES F. STANLEY

ZONDERVAN
BOOKS

ZONDERVAN BOOKS

When You Don't Know What to Pray
Copyright © 2021 by Charles F. Stanley

Requests for information should be addressed to:
Zondervan, *3900 Sparks Dr. SE, Grand Rapids, Michigan 49546*

Zondervan titles may be purchased in bulk for educational, business, fundraising, or sales promotional use. For information, please email SpecialMarkets@Zondervan.com.

ISBN 978-0-310-36079-7 (audio)

Library of Congress Cataloging-in-Publication Data

Names: Stanley, Charles F., author.
Title: When you don't know what to pray : 100 essential prayers for enduring life's storms / Charles F. Stanley.
Description: Grand Rapids : Zondervan, 2021. | Summary: "God longs to interact with us and help us with our burdens, but many of us struggle to translate our pain, desires, and hopes into words. In this book, internationally respected pastor and bestselling author Dr. Charles Stanley offers 100 heartfelt, powerful prayers that will transform your life and deepen your communion with Christ"— Provided by publisher.
Identifiers: LCCN 2020037040 (print) | LCCN 2020037041 (ebook) | ISBN 9780310360773 (hardcover) | ISBN 9780310360780 (ebook)
Subjects: LCSH: Prayers. | Prayer—Christianity.
Classification: LCC BV245 .S648 2021 (print) | LCC BV245 (ebook) | DDC 242/.4—dc23
LC record available at https://lccn.loc.gov/2020037040
LC ebook record available at https://lccn.loc.gov/2020037041

Cover design: Curt Diepenhorst
Cover image: darekm101 / Getty Images
Interior design: Kait Lamphere

Printed in the United States of America

21 22 23 24 25 26 27 28 29 30 31 32 /LSC/ 16 15 14 13 12 11 10 9 8 7 6 5 4 3 2 1

CONTENTS

Section 1
PRAYERS FOR WHEN
EMOTIONS TAKE OVER

Section 2
PRAYERS FOR WHEN
LIFE IS DIFFICULT

Section 3
PRAYERS FOR WHEN
OTHERS NEED HELP

Section 4
PRAYERS FOR WHEN
YOU FEEL CALLED

INTRODUCTION

The Spirit also helps our weakness; for we do not know how to pray as we should, but the Spirit Himself intercedes for us with groanings too deep for words; and He who searches the hearts knows what the mind of the Spirit is, because He intercedes for the saints according to the will of God.

—ROMANS 8:26–27

Prayer. It is the awesome gift that connects us to the living God—to the One who is able by His wisdom, power, and love to help us through whatever we face.

We know God is there for us, just waiting for us to approach His throne and present our burdened hearts to His care. We have learned this as a principle taught in Scripture—as what we are supposed to believe with our minds and hearts. The problem is, sometimes we don't *feel* it—we are unsure whether what we articulate will make a difference to the Lord. We want to trust Him—we want Him to intervene in our circumstances. But our doubts and insecurities about our own failings and limitations can take over. So we experience trouble even knowing what to say to Him.

At these times, we may feel somewhat lost about how to express the full depth of our desires or feelings to God. Perhaps we realize we don't fully understand what we truly need, much less how to verbalize it. There may even be moments when we are so exhausted and confused—in spirit, mind, and body—that we can hardly muster the energy to open our mouths. Perhaps discouragement has taken such a strong hold of us that we can't imagine a way out of our painful circumstances, and all we can do is entreat the Father to help us.

Thankfully, Scripture promises the Holy Spirit's help at those moments (see Romans 8:26–27). And I believe that wholeheartedly. I know that the Holy Spirit teaches us how and what to pray in accordance with what the Father desires for us. So be assured, the Lord Himself will help you communicate with Him. That is how deeply He wants a relationship with you and for you to entrust your life to His care.

My prayer is that this book will help you hear how the Holy Spirit works through God's Word to communicate to you, that you'll be prompted to pray in agreement with Him, and that you will overcome the hurdles you face in walking with your Savior. This book is not intended to take His place in your life, by any means. So please don't expect these to be magical prayers or a guidebook on how to get what you want from the Lord. On the contrary, the goal is for you to hear Jesus—to know Him better and love Him more in the distinct area where you are enduring a storm.

When you struggle in what to say to God, take these words as an example of how to pour out your heart to Him. And as you read these prayers, make them your own. Listen to what the Lord God is saying. As Scripture comes to mind, pray that too. Allow God to speak to you, heal you, and lead you in the way you should go. Learn to talk to and interact with your Savior. And may you experience the great joy and deep comfort of trusting Him through life's every struggle, and the awesome victory of winning your battles on your knees with Him.

Lord Jesus, how grateful I am for the privilege of prayer—for the ability to communicate with You at any and every moment. Help me to pray and to be assured of Your salvation and presence. You are my Savior now and forever. You promise in Your Word that nothing can ever separate me from Your love (Romans 8:38–39). You have guaranteed that when I seek You, I will find You, that when I pray, You hear me. Thank You for always being with me. How grateful I am that You show me how to rely on You through the storms and challenges of life and for the amazing depth of Your comfort and care.

I believe You, Lord Jesus; please help my unbelief. I need to trust You more—to know that it is not the eloquence of my words but the depth of Your great love and provision that give power to my prayers. So please teach me to pray, Lord Jesus. Show me how to be in constant fellowship with You.

Pray through me, Holy Spirit—give me the words that will express my heart and exalt the Lord my God. Bring Scripture to mind that I can claim. Help me to know You and love You more, my Savior. Speak to me, heal me, and lead me to walk in the center of Your will. Thank You, Lord, for helping me to hear what You are saying and to see how You are working in my situation.

In Jesus's name I pray. Amen.

WHEN YOU WANT
to Accept Jesus as Your Savior

If you confess with your mouth Jesus as Lord, and believe in your heart that God raised Him from the dead, you will be saved.
—ROMANS 10:9

Lord Jesus, I come before You in humility and repentance, realizing that there is no way I can pay for my sin or earn my way to a relationship with God. I understand my good works will never be enough. But You say in Your Word that You offer me salvation as a gracious gift that I can accept by faith (Ephesians 2:8–9). Therefore, Lord Jesus, by faith I accept Your death on the cross as sufficient payment for my sins and the way to be reconciled to the Father.

Lord, I confess that I have violated Your holy laws and fall short of the purposes for which You created me. Please forgive my sins and save me from eternal separation from You. Jesus, I receive You as my personal Savior and Lord, fully trusting in the work You accomplished once and for all on my behalf through Your death and resurrection.

Thank You, Jesus, for providing the way to know You and to have everlasting life. Thank You for saving me, accepting me, and adopting me into Your family. Thank You for giving me the Holy Spirit to indwell me, lead me in Your truth, and seal me for the day of redemption.

Jesus, please help me live in a personal, intimate relationship with You from now on and confess You as my Lord by obeying what You ask. Please give me the strength, wisdom, and determination to walk in the center of Your will from now on. Thank You for hearing my prayers and loving me unconditionally.

In Jesus's name I pray. Amen.

RECORD YOUR DECISION

If you have just accepted Jesus as your Savior, write down your decision so you'll never doubt Jesus has truly given you eternal life and a home in heaven forever:

I, _____, accepted Jesus as my Lord and
[name]

Savior on _____, and nothing can separate me
[date]

from His love ever again (Romans 8:38–39).

Section 1

PRAYERS FOR
WHEN EMOTIONS
TAKE OVER

WHEN YOU ARE *Afraid*

Fear not, for I am with you;
Be not dismayed, for I am your God.
I will strengthen you,
Yes, I will help you,
I will uphold you with My righteous right hand.
—ISAIAH 41:10 NKJV

Father, how grateful I am for Your awesome love and that You are with me at this moment when I need the comfort only You can provide.

I am afraid. I am shaken to my core. But You know all about my fears—how deeply they affect me, where they originate in my heart and mind, and how they ultimately paralyze me from moving forward in important ways. Thank You, Father, for helping me overcome the things I am afraid of and offering me Your peace and security.

Father, it is amazing how situations such as the one I am facing can knock me off my feet and throw me off balance. I know that happens because I feel weak and frightened when I lack control. However, I recognize that when I wrestle with such fears, they ultimately exist because of what I believe about You. I am focused on myself and the challenges rather than You. Therefore, please reveal where my fears have taken root and why they exist. Lord, remove the lies I believe and the issues that prevent me from fully embracing who You are. Continue to give me strength and courage through Your Word. Comfort me with Your nearness, and reassure me of Your constant presence. Teach me about who You are so I can stand strong against these fears and declare in faith, "My God is wiser, more loving, and more powerful than any problem I could ever face!" Help me to daily place my focus on Your unfailing character and life-giving principles so that I can be courageous—a person who obeys and pleases You in every way.

Father, I am grateful that You want me to be free and won't let me remain in bondage—You don't want me to be a slave to my fears. You desire for me to enjoy the abundant life You created me for. Therefore, You bring my fears to light so that You can deliver me from them and I can be free.

So I will set my heart to believe You and will say as David did,

> Whenever I am afraid,
> I will trust in You.
> In God (I will praise His word),
> In God I have put my trust;
> I will not fear.
> What can flesh do to me? . . .
> In God I have put my trust;
> I will not be afraid.
> What can man do to me? . . .
> For You have delivered my soul from death.
> Have You not kept my feet from falling,
> That I may walk before God
> In the light of the living? (Psalm 56:3–4, 11, 13 NKJV)

I bless and praise You for Your kindness and the patience with which You heal my wounds. Thank You, Father, that I can have victory over my fears because of who You are and what You've promised. You said I can have confidence because You will be my God, You will always be with me, and You will protect me with Your righteous right hand.

You are the all-powerful and all-wise God who defends me. Truly, You are worthy of all the honor, glory, power, and praise! And my soul rests secure and in peace because of You.

In Jesus's name I pray. Amen.

WHEN YOU ARE
Angry

*"In your anger do not sin": Do not let the sun go down while you
are still angry, and do not give the devil a foothold.*
—EPHESIANS 4:26–27 NIV

Father, please calm me at this moment when anger has taken hold
of me. I know You call me to release it and forgive, but I need You to
help me do so. How grateful I am that You are patient, loving, kind,
and forgiving toward me. You have many more reasons to be angry
than I ever do, yet You always look to me with compassion, grace, and
mercy. Please help me to be more like You—in word, thought, and deed.

Lord, I confess my anger today and ask You to please cleanse my
heart of the deep resentment, bitterness, and injury I feel. They run so
deep, Father—and the strength of those feelings alarms me at times.
I know that this situation is not only about how I was wronged or
the person who hurt me. It touched a profound place within me that
needs healing, which is why this person's actions provoked me so
completely. Please show me where this pain originates from, and root
it out of my soul so that I will not sin against You. When I am angry,
reveal constructive and loving ways to deal with my emotions—giving
me the patience and wisdom to pause and deal with what is really
going on, rather than just lashing out.

Please help me to forgive as You do, Jesus, knowing that I can trust
You to bring justice and healing in this situation. Show me Your divine
perspective of this person and situation so I can have compassion and

can extend grace. Jesus, as the Roman soldiers nailed You to the cross, You said, "Father, forgive them; for they do not know what they are doing" (Luke 23:34). I know that is the kind of heart You call me to have. Even if the person who wounded me knows some of what they have done, I realize that a broken part of them is blind to why they commit these actions. So I pray You would reveal Yourself to them powerfully—leading them to a deeper relationship with You, healing the wounds of their heart and working reconciliation in and through these circumstances. Father, please help me to be like You—loving and holy, forgiving even when it is difficult, understanding that this person does not recognize the full extent of their actions or the profound brokenness that motivates them. Give me spiritual eyes to see how I can be Your agent of grace in their life.

I know that nothing passes through Your hand and touches my life without some purpose. So whether You are revealing my woundedness, leading me to forgive, or teaching some other lesson that will help me become more like You, please make it known to me, Father. I want to learn all You have to teach me. I want to be a person of peace and grace, reflecting the very character of Jesus. Father, please help me understand why certain traps entangle me and how I can be free of them. And show me, my Savior, how I can be Your representative—helping others to be liberated from their anger and leading them to faith in You.

In Jesus's name I pray. Amen.

WHEN YOU ARE
Anxious

Be anxious for nothing, but in everything by prayer and supplication with thanksgiving let your requests be made known to God. And the peace of God, which surpasses all comprehension, will guard your hearts and your minds in Christ Jesus.
—PHILIPPIANS 4:6–7

Father, I come before You today with anxiety on my heart. The what-ifs are overwhelming me. At times, this uneasiness strikes me in a manner that consumes my thoughts and paralyzes me from going forward. I can't break free of this apprehension on my own. Although there are real issues that cause me concern and contribute to my apprehension, I find that what I really dread are the dark unknowns ahead of me.

But, Father, this I call to mind, and therefore I have hope: You hold my future in Your hands and nothing can thwart Your purposes for me. How grateful I am that the days ahead belong to You. Thank You for working to set me free from this bondage to anxiety by bringing my true concerns to light. I bring all my soul dreads to You. You know what really consumes me and dominates my thoughts—the coping mechanisms and false beliefs that keep me fearful. Thank You for revealing those wounded, unhealthy, broken places within me and for Your liberating love and grace that empower me to overcome, even right now. Thank You for teaching me the truth by which I can be set free.

Lord, I acknowledge that, ultimately, what I am facing is a faith battle and that a great deal of what I struggle with comes down to what I believe about You. Likewise, it is possible that some of my anxiety originates from negative interactions with authority figures and experiences early in my life that have influenced how I view You. Father, I want to know who You truly are. Reveal Yourself to me through Your Word. Lord, where I have any wrong perceptions of Your character or intentions—please drive them out. Help me to see You as my perfect security, identity, and the highest goal of my life. I know that when I trust in You, I will never be disappointed.

Therefore, I declare once and for all that I believe You. I have faith that You are greater, stronger, and more powerful than any problem I could ever face. Thank You for being my Father, understanding my situation, and caring enough to help me in every circumstance. I am grateful that this situation will help me know You better, that You will always show me what to do, and that You will guide me in the best way possible. So I give all my concerns to You and trust that You have already given me the victory through the Lord Jesus. I am so grateful that You love me unconditionally, have promised to provide for me, and have the wisdom and strength necessary to break me free of this bondage to anxiety.

Thank You, Father, that Your healing in me has begun. Continue to draw me to Yourself, empowering me with Your courage and restoring me by your love and wisdom. Through the work of Your Holy Spirit, expose what is hidden, repair what has been broken, and make me into everything You purposed I would be when You formed me. I commit my life to Your loving care and faithful stewardship, knowing You have never let me down and never will. I bless and praise You for Your kindness and the patience with which You teach me to walk in Your will. Thank You for giving me the peace that passes understanding in all that concerns me.

In Jesus's name I pray. Amen.

WHEN YOU ARE
Bitter

*Let all bitterness and wrath and anger and clamor and slander
be put away from you, along with all malice. Be kind to one
another, tender-hearted, forgiving each other, just as God in
Christ also has forgiven you.*
—EPHESIANS 4:31–32

Father, my soul is burdened with bitterness. I know it because of
the anger that infects my life and interactions with others. I am broken before You, burdened and defeated because of this resentment
within me. I kneel before Your throne and ask for what I have not
been strong enough to give—grace. I know this bitterness within me
is a serious offense in Your eyes, and I accept full responsibility for the
unforgiveness that I've allowed to live within my heart. Please forgive
me, Father. Show me how to lay down the blame for my wounds. Even
in the places where I feel my hurt is valid, please help me to let go of the
offenses against me. Send Your Holy Spirit to teach me how to truly
forgive so I can be free from this bondage to bitterness and resentment and be healed fully. And please, Father, restore the relationships
that have been unwittingly hurt due to my stubbornness.

You have forgiven me of so much, Jesus. When I think of it all,
I am overwhelmed by Your mercy toward me. Thank You so much
for Your amazing grace. I want to have Your heart for others so that
they will see You in me. Therefore, Lord, even though it is difficult,
I pray for the people who have hurt me. Lord, I know that I may think

I understand what caused them to do as they did, but I confess that my comprehension is incomplete and may even be faulty. So please, Father, open my eyes and help me to see what is really going on. Show me their hearts, Father—what wounds, misunderstandings, and bondage keep them bound—and fill me with Your grace for them. Help me to have mercy for them, and show me how to demonstrate Your love and compassion to them in a way that is meaningful and glorifies You. Please draw them into a deeper relationship with You, healing any woundedness in their hearts and revealing Yourself to them.

Please restore me as well, Father. Convict me of my own sin, and show me how to repent completely. Let nothing remain unexamined in my life. Whenever I am tempted to resent others or slide back into bitterness, remind me of 1 John 4:20, "If someone says, 'I love God,' and hates his brother, he is a liar; for the one who does not love his brother whom he has seen, cannot love God whom he has not seen." I realize You know every person and circumstance that has touched my life and that You have seen it all. Because You could have prevented what wounded me, my bitterness really isn't at others; it's at You. So please help me to see the people who hurt me as tools in Your hand for good—to grow my heart to better know Yours, to develop my spiritual life, and to accomplish Your purposes. Make me more sensitive to all You desire to teach me.

Father, thank You that when I stumble and fall, You pick me up. I am so grateful that You show me how to be free of bitterness. Help me to live a life worthy of Your name. Thank You for softening and cleansing my heart, liberating me from unforgiveness, and leading me in the work of restoring the relationships I have damaged because of my woundedness. Thank You for not giving up on me. Truly, no one is more gracious, loving, merciful, or compassionate than You are.

In Jesus's name I pray. Amen.

WHEN YOU ARE
Confused

Trust in the LORD with all your heart
And do not lean on your own understanding.
In all your ways acknowledge Him,
And He will make your paths straight.
—PROVERBS 3:5–6

Lord Jesus, I confess that I don't know what to do and can't wrap my mind around the circumstances before me. Something is missing in my understanding of the situation. I can't see Your hand, and the actions of others have perplexed me.

Father, I need Your help. I claim Your promise: "If any of you lacks wisdom, let him ask of God, who gives to all generously and without reproach, and it will be given to him" (James 1:5). Lord Jesus, I need Your lavish wisdom. You understand all things and see every aspect of my dilemma—even the facts and forces that I do not know exist. You see the holes in my comprehension, the issues I am blind to, the perfect course to take, and how this will affect my future. You have formed the hearts of all involved and comprehend all their wounds and workings.

I think of Paul's words in Romans 11:33: "Oh, the depth of the riches both of the wisdom and knowledge of God! How unsearchable are His judgments and unfathomable His ways!" That is who You are, Lord. In wisdom You have created all things. You see the end from the beginning. You are never confused. You are never without perfect understanding, regardless of what happens.

Father, You know what to do. My circumstances neither surprise nor perplex You. Therefore, my Lord, Savior, Provider, and mighty Defender, open Your Word to me, make it a lamp to my feet and a light to my path. If my plans clash with Yours, I declare right now, "Your will be done." If the purpose of this season of confusion is so I will learn to lean not on my own understanding but to follow You more closely, then I proclaim, "Here I am, Lord. Your servant is listening." If this is to build my faith, I say, "I believe, Jesus; help my unbelief."

Whatever Your purpose for this season, I seek You with all my heart and submit to You completely, with full confidence that You will lead me along the path of life and in the center of Your perfect will. Thank You for loving me, giving me insight into this situation, and showing me what to do.

In Jesus's name I pray. Amen.

WHEN YOU ARE
Discouraged

They trusted and You delivered them.
To You they cried out and were delivered;
In You they trusted and were not disappointed.
—PSALM 22:4-5

Jesus, I confess these are the moments that make it difficult to find hope and keep pressing on. I know I should always feel confident about the future because You are in my life and always have a good plan. But the emotions I am experiencing because of this disappointment are so great. It has brought up other unhealed disillusionment and regrets deep in my heart that have piled one on another, compounding what I am feeling right now. Help me, my Savior.

I know that at these times, the best thing I can do is worship You. I recognize that my misplaced focus is causing the struggle I am facing—my attention is on my problems, rather than on Your perfect provision. Therefore, I fix my eyes on You, Jesus—the author and perfecter of my faith. You are all-knowing, all-powerful, and have even overcome the grave! Nothing is too difficult for You—including the obstacles before me. How grateful I am for Your awesome love and good, pleasing, and acceptable plan for me.

Jesus, I even thank You for this discouragement, realizing You are using it for Your purposes. You know all about my fears and surface them so I will take hold of Your peace that passes understanding, which is founded in Your perfect wisdom and unfathomable power.

I am so grateful that You reveal where my discouragement comes from—the false beliefs and wounds that exacerbate it—so it all can be completely removed. Thank You for teaching me how to overcome the things I am afraid of, for giving me courage, and for leading me to victory.

Therefore, Lord, whenever I am discouraged, immediately draw me into Your presence and remind me to seek You in prayer. Teach me about who You are. Fill me with courage through my growing relationship with You. Reveal promises from Your Word that I can hold on to. Strengthen my faith and transform my mind so I can stand steadfast against disappointments and declare with full confidence, "My God is greater than any problem I will ever face, and He will help me through!" Day by day, show me how to place my focus on Your faithful character and unfailing principles. Guide me so I can become a person of courage and conviction, who obeys, pleases You, and becomes all You created me to be. Train me to praise You in every circumstance, my God. Whenever I speak defeatist words of worry or faithlessness, convict me of it, Lord, so I can change what I am expressing. In every way, help me to always glorify You with my conversation.

Thank You, Father, that I don't have to give in to my disappointments because of who You are and what You've promised me. You said, "Do not fear, for I am with you; do not anxiously look about you, for I am your God. I will strengthen you, surely I will help you, surely I will uphold you with My righteous right hand" (Isaiah 41:10). Therefore, I set my heart to take courage and will not be afraid. Truly, You are worthy of all the honor, glory, power, and praise! I will rest in You, because You, Father, are trustworthy and give peace to my soul.

In Jesus's name I pray. Amen.

WHEN YOU ARE
Grieving

The LORD has heard the voice of my weeping.
The LORD has heard my supplication,
The LORD receives my prayer.

—PSALM 6:8–9

Oh, Lord Jesus, how deep is my anguish at this loss. I bring it to You, grateful that You promise to share in my sorrow and soothe my soul. I take comfort in knowing that You understand exactly how I feel since You experienced the full impact of grief at Gethsemane. How I identify with Your words: "My soul is deeply grieved, to the point of death" (Matthew 26:38).

This hurts so deeply, Jesus, and I have many unanswered questions. I realize I can't stifle this agony, because that will only complicate this already difficult situation. So I ask You to please help me express this pain in healthy ways. I confess that my emotions are overloaded, my mind feels like it is in a fog, and even my body is wracked by this loss. I am weary and having trouble taking it all in. I don't know what to do. I don't know how to go forward.

Father, they say this is all normal after a great loss. I realize I need to take time to process all that has happened. So, Lord, please teach me to be patient with myself and be steadfast in clinging to You. Protect me from the pressure to move on too quickly or to expect more from myself than I need to—especially when it comes to making big decisions. But also, Father, don't allow me to give in to unforgiveness, guilt, anger, despair, or self-destruction. I know I will be tempted to drown out this pain. Instead, help me face it with Your grace and wisdom so I can be healed and learn from it.

Father, right now, it doesn't feel like there's much light on my horizon, but I cling to the fact that I can always hope in You. I don't know why You allowed this great pain in my life. It seems so unfair. But I realize that from Your heavenly perspective, You see an important reason. I submit to You in this, knowing Your will is good, acceptable, and perfect. So comfort my heart and teach me, Jesus. Send me Your people to help me and show me who to confide in. I thank You for catching my tears, being near to those whose hearts are broken, and saving the crushed in spirit.

Glorify Yourself in this situation, Lord. If this can make me more useful for Your kingdom, or strengthen my faith and character, or can result in ministry to others, I will have reason to rejoice. Thank You for never leaving or forsaking me. Thank You for hearing my prayer and comforting me in this hour of need.

In Jesus's name I pray. Amen.

WHEN YOU ARE
Hurt

We do not have a high priest who cannot sympathize with our weaknesses, but One who has been tempted in all things as we are, yet without sin. Therefore let us draw near with confidence to the throne of grace, so that we may receive mercy and find grace to help in time of need.

—HEBREWS 4:15–16

Lord, I come before You with a deep hurt that persists within me. Father, how thankful I am that You know all about it, where it comes from, and how to help my aching heart. I have nowhere to go but to You. When I have tried to communicate what I am going through, others often just don't understand and sometimes even condemn or criticize me as I try to work out what is happening. And as You know, Father, I simply can't share all there is to it. Some things I can't verbalize because of how deep they go, how private they are, and how they affect others. It all makes me feel so isolated in this pain.

But, Father, I am so grateful that You know. My soul and my situation are laid bare before You. Nothing is hidden from Your sight. Thank You for caring for me in my distress, understanding it fully, and accepting even the most profoundly wounded parts of me. I am so grateful I don't have to feel shame in Your loving presence. Yes, You convict me of sin—but not to condemn. Rather, You do so to set me free of all that keeps me in bondage. I am grateful that Your desire is to heal me, Lord.

So, Lord Jesus, my High Priest, Deliverer, Defender, and Great Physician, examine me and soothe this pain within me. Mend what is broken, and reveal the ways I perpetuate this distress through my thoughts, beliefs, and actions so I can repent and seek Your forgiveness. Likewise, help me to forgive myself and others. Show me where I have accepted lies, and replace them with Your truth. I submit myself to You.

It is time for true recovery to begin—and that comes through You, Lord Jesus. Thank You for Your compassion, kindness, and love. Thank You that I can always approach Your throne of grace and find the mercy and help I need. Thank You, Lord Jesus, that You know even better than I do how I feel and are always willing to help me.

In Jesus's name I pray. Amen.

WHEN YOU ARE
Jealous

Delight yourself in the LORD;
And He will give you the desires of your heart.
Commit your way to the LORD,
Trust also in Him, and He will do it.

—PSALM 37:4–5

Father, I feel jealous today. I don't understand why You chose to give the blessing I so desperately desired to another person and not to me. In my mind, I trust that You have Your good reasons. But in my heart, it hurts and feels so unfair. I don't want to be the kind of person who doubts You or who feels displeasure upon seeing another's good fortune. Please help me, Lord Jesus.

I thank You, Father, for surfacing these feelings so I can truly see what is in my heart. I see how destructive this is in me. This is stealing my peace because I am fixing my focus on blessings and on other people rather than on You. So I confess this jealousy and ask You to show me how to be free of it. Do not allow me to become bound by a spirit of self-pity, self-condemnation, comparison, insecurity, or criticism of others—all of which do not fit me as Your child. Likewise, Father, if there is any pride or selfishness in me, reveal it and remove it. Forgive me for any way I have been resentful or have displeased You with my actions.

Thank You, Lord, for loving me and being understanding about where I am in my walk with You but not allowing me to remain stuck in destructive thought patterns, attitudes, and habits. Thank You for blessing others and, through that, reminding me that every good thing given and every perfect gift is from You. I confess my trust in Your wisdom and timing. Give me love for those who possess what I desire, rather than jealousy. Help me learn what You are teaching, and keep my focus on You, Lord Jesus. I will delight myself in You, Lord; knowing You will bless me in a manner that truly ministers to my soul. I commit my way to You, Lord, with full faith that You will accomplish all that concerns me. Thank You, my Savior. I praise Your holy name.

In Jesus's name I pray. Amen.

WHEN YOU FEAR
the Future

*"I know the plans that I have for you," declares the L*ORD*, "plans for welfare and not for calamity to give you a future and a hope."*
—JEREMIAH 29:11

Lord God, I come before You today because I am confused and fearful about the future. The events that have transpired have caused me to question the path before me. But, Father, how thankful I am that You rule all things from heaven. You are holy and exalted—wise and good in all You do. I know, even though from my perspective the days ahead appear dark, that You have looked ahead and know the way I should take. Thank You for Your wonderful plan for my life and that even the setbacks I encounter can't stop what You have purposed for me—but rather they serve Your plan in some important manner.

Lord, I am grateful that my future originates and is found at Your throne. I know You speak and make a way for me. You command, and closed doors are opened in a manner that no one can shut them. Help me listen to You reflectively, actively, submissively, expectantly, and patiently. When I can't hear Your voice, give me the endurance to keep seeking You and Your will. I acknowledge You as my Lord in all things; guide me and make my way straight.

Jesus, thank You for all You do on my behalf. I thank You for my daily bread and that You take care of all my needs—even the ones that appear unmet at the moment. Thank You for pardoning my sins and helping me forgive those who hurt me. Thank You for helping me fight and escape temptation so I can live a holy life that honors You. Thank You for delivering me from evil and from the bondage to sin.

Father, may Your gospel be preached throughout the earth, and may people acknowledge that You are the King of Kings and the Lord of Lords. May every knee bow, and may every tongue confess that Jesus is Lord. May Your will be done—on earth as it is in heaven—especially in and through my life. Continue to show me how I can join You in Your purposes and be a living, active, productive member of the body of Christ.

For Yours is the kingdom and the power and the glory forever, Lord Jesus. You are my Savior, Authority, Defender, and Great Provider. Because of You, I can look forward to the future with joy, expectation, and anticipation, knowing that You lead me perfectly and are worthy of all my respect, worship, obedience, and adoration. Thank You for leading me to life at its best. To You be all glory, honor, and praise forever.

In Jesus's name I pray. Amen.

WHEN YOU FEEL
Alone

The LORD is the one who goes ahead of you; He will be with you.
He will not fail you or forsake you. Do not fear or be dismayed.
—DEUTERONOMY 31:8

Lord, thank You for being with me in this difficult moment. Father, I am so glad that You never leave or forsake me, regardless of what happens. You are my Rock, Redeemer, and Shelter. Nothing can take me out of Your hand or separate me from Your love. That is what Your Word says, Father. That is what You have promised me. And I claim it as true right now, because the truth is that I feel as if I am completely and utterly alone. I don't sense Your presence—it's as if You are a million miles away. So I cling to Your promises by faith because that is what You've told me to do.

Jesus, please make Yourself known and comfort me. You are my Savior. You made Your great sacrifice on the cross to reconcile me to Yourself forever. Your resurrection proved once and for all that I have a living relationship with You that nothing—not even sin or death—could hinder. While I was still a sinner, You died for me. You accepted me at my worst, and You continue to receive me now. Even when I feel like no one understands me, You do—even better than I do myself. I praise You for Your amazing kindness and sacrificial grace, Jesus. Thank You for loving me so much and so unconditionally.

Lord, I realize that loneliness can have many different sources, including how I have been rejected, shamed, alienated, and betrayed in the past and how I have isolated myself as a result. But in some ways, my loneliness stems from not understanding how to love others or to receive love. Teach me, Lord. Heal the wounds of the past, and help me forgive those who've hurt me. Show me how to walk in healthy relationship with You and with others. Reveal to me the people You desire me to reach out to and care about. And help me appreciate and cherish the people You have given to love me—rather than chasing after the approval of those who don't.

Lord Jesus, You said You would not leave me as an orphan, and You are always with me through the presence of Your Holy Spirit. Thank You that I don't walk through this life alone and misunderstood but always have Your everlasting arms to lean upon. What great comfort and strength You give me to endure today and every day. Thank You for leading me out of the pain of loneliness and being my constant, everlasting Companion.

In Jesus's name I pray. Amen.

WHEN YOU FEEL
Despair

We do not want you to be unaware, brethren, of our affliction which came to us in Asia, that we were burdened excessively, beyond our strength, so that we despaired even of life; indeed, we had the sentence of death within ourselves so that we would not trust in ourselves, but in God who raises the dead.

—2 CORINTHIANS 1:8–9

Father, how grateful I am that You understand when I feel depressed and utterly hopeless. Even at this moment, I come to You in despondency, not knowing how I can possibly continue. You know how the circumstances and problems I have faced over the years have made me feel like I am unworthy—like a thick cloak of darkness has settled on my life. I thank You for giving me light and always reminding me that no matter what happens or what anyone says, You call me accepted and worthy—Your beloved child.

Lord God, I give thanks for Your consistent tenderness toward me, the way You give me hope, and how You work to heal my wounds. You know, Lord, how I can become discouraged. I realize that the trials You send to draw me closer to You build my faith, set me free from bondage, establish my character, and help me embrace Your true resurrection life. But they hit the wounded parts in me that make me feel like I have no hope. So, Father, whenever I feel despair taking hold of me, help me remember to kneel before You in prayer and to seek Your loving face. I know You are trying to shake me free from my old ways so I can walk in Yours. In those moments, lead me to focus on Your matchless character, remind me of Your plans for my future, and strengthen me so I can persevere in my commitment to You. Help me embrace the good works You have prepared in advance for me to do and who You've created me to be (Ephesians 2:10). May Your praises always be on my lips, because I know that is the way to true life and healing.

Lord, what always gives my heart hope most is to remember who You are and the great love You always show me. Truly, You are God—the good, holy, sovereign, compassionate, and trustworthy God of all that exists. You are clothed with majesty and strength. Your wisdom none can fathom. Your astounding mercy, amazing grace, and unconditional love cause me to rejoice. When I look to You, I remember that my situation is never truly hopeless—that deliverance will come when Your purposes are accomplished.

Thank You, Father, for giving me hope. I am so grateful that You lead me to victory over my despair. Indeed, Lord, You make the disappointments of my life into a classroom where I can grow closer to You and learn to take hold of every blessing You have for me. Even when troubles surround me, circumstances rise up against me, and there's no rescue in view, I know You are with me. You act powerfully on my behalf in the unseen, and I have confidence that I will see You work everything together for good. Truly, Your great and mighty plans are above and beyond all I could possibly ask or imagine. So help me reflect Your glory, Father, leading others to know You and helping them to find healing in Your wise and loving presence.

In Jesus's name I pray. Amen.

WHEN YOU FEEL
God Is Distant

O Lord, be not far off;
O You my help, hasten to my assistance . . .
You who fear the Lord, praise Him;
All you descendants of Jacob, glorify Him,
And stand in awe of Him, all you descendants of Israel.
For He has not despised nor abhorred the affliction of the afflicted;
Nor has He hidden His face from him;
But when he cried to Him for help, He heard.
                    —PSALM 22:19, 23–24

Father, I feel so distant from You, and I'm not sure what to do about it. I realize that every believer has times when You seem far off—desert times when we must choose to believe Your promise to always be with us, rather than trusting our feelings. But, Jesus, I long for Your presence with me. I need Your comfort, wisdom, and strength. I cry out as David did, "O my God, do not be far from me! Make haste to help me, O Lord, my salvation!" (Psalm 38:21–22). Just as David was reassured that You heard him, I ask that You would help me be confident of Your presence as well, whether that be through Your Word, a memory of Your intervention, a friend, a song, a sermon, or whatever You choose to use.

Father, if there is some sin in me that is separating me from You, please show me so I can confess it and repent from it. If I am believing a lie of the Enemy that is undermining my relationship with You, purge it out and lead me in Your truth. And if there is something You are teaching me, Father, help me learn it quickly so I can again enjoy a close, intimate walk with You.

I cry out to You, Lord, grateful that You always hear me and always answer. I'm so glad You never leave or forsake me and that this distance is only a feeling, not the reality of our relationship. Thank You for showing me the cause of this distance and helping me surmount it. Thank You for opening Your Word, speaking to me through Your Holy Spirit, and restoring our sweet fellowship. I set my heart to listen to You, my Lord God. Thank You for communicating with me and drawing me close once again.

In Jesus's name I pray. Amen.

WHEN YOU FEEL
Empty

Whoever drinks of the water that I will give him shall never thirst; but the water that I will give him will become in him a well of water springing up to eternal life.

—JOHN 4:14

Father, I feel so empty in many different ways. I feel as if nothing is filling my heart, spirit, and soul. Something is missing—something is off and incomplete. There is no real peace or joy; there is just numbness within me. It seems as if I have lost my purpose, direction, and passion. Lord God, You have promised to fill me up—to give me Your abundant life if I will allow You to. Therefore, Father, I present my heart to You and ask that You remove anything that stands in the way of me experiencing the overflowing Christian life You intended me to have.

Father, I confess I have tried to fill my life with what I thought would give me pleasure and comfort but has left me hollow. I'm guilty of the admonishment You proclaimed through the prophet Jeremiah: "They have forsaken Me, the fountain of living waters, to hew for themselves cisterns, broken cisterns that can hold no water" (Jeremiah 2:13). What I have looked to for consolation has left me even emptier and more convinced of my own worthlessness. It has not worked but has worn away at who You created me to be. Show me all the ways I have turned away from You so I can confess them, find Your forgiveness, and begin to walk according to Your will. Let none of it remain.

Father, I would also ask You to show me how to make You my fountain of living water. Speak powerfully and clearly through Your Word as I kneel before You in prayer. Send believers who understand how to live the abundant Christian life to help me take hold of it. Live Your life through me, my Lord and my Savior. I don't know all that means, but my heart is open before You, and I'm willing to learn whatever You desire to teach me.

Thank You, Father, for genuinely loving, accepting, and caring for me. Thank You for seeing my life as more than it presently is and for having greater plans than I can imagine. You have dreams for me, Father—better ones than I have for myself—and You empower me to take hold of them. Thank You, Lord. Show me what is possible. Fill me up as I find true joy and acceptance in Your presence. And may my life become a testimony of the fullness of a powerful, intimate relationship with You that will give others hope as well.

In Jesus's name I pray. Amen.

WHEN YOU FEEL
Guilt

I acknowledged my sin to You,
And my iniquity I did not hide;
I said, "I will confess my transgressions to the LORD";
And You forgave the guilt of my sin.   Selah.
Therefore, let everyone who is godly pray to You in a time when
      You may be found;
Surely in a flood of great waters they will not reach him.
You are my hiding place; You preserve me from trouble;
You surround me with songs of deliverance.   Selah.

—PSALM 32:5-7

Father, I feel such guilt over the things I have done. I know I have confessed them to You as fully as I know how and that You have forgiven me. But for some reason it gnaws at me, as if there is still something wrong. So, Father, I ask You right now, reveal anything I still need to confess so that I can repent and follow You fully. I submit myself to You, Lord, wholeheartedly longing to obey You and be free from this reproach.

Thank You for being faithful to forgive my sins. As I confess my transgressions to You and repent from them, You cleanse me from unrighteousness. I am so grateful that because of the substitutionary death of Christ on the cross, I can never lose my relationship with You. It is so comforting to know that You will always love me, no matter what.

34

Lord, I am so grateful that You do not want me to suffer from false guilt; rather, You want to free me from it and love me unconditionally. Father, when I feel false guilt, please reveal the cause of it so that it can be unearthed and removed. I don't want to sin, Jesus, so when I stray from the center of Your will, convict me of it powerfully, without delay, so I may repent of it immediately—turning back to Your perfect plan. Lord, I choose to believe that You forgive me fully and perfectly, despite however I might feel. Help me accept any consequences of my sin and grow through the discipline You send.

Lord God, I know You cause "all things to work together for good to those who love [You], to those who are called according to [Your] purpose" (Romans 8:28). Therefore, Father, please help me learn from my mistakes. Then, as David says, "I will teach your ways to other sinners, and they—guilty like me—will repent and return to you" (Psalm 51:13 TLB). Lord God, make me an instrument of Your peace to others so that they will know Jesus as their Savior and find the true freedom from their sins that only You can give.

In Jesus's name I pray. Amen.

WHEN YOU FEEL
Humiliated

All day long my dishonor is before me
And my humiliation has overwhelmed me. . . .
But we have not forgotten You,
And we have not dealt falsely with Your covenant.
Our heart has not turned back,
And our steps have not deviated from Your way. . . .
Rise up, be our help,
And redeem us for the sake of Your lovingkindness.

—PSALM 44:15, 17–18, 26

Father, how grateful I am that You always receive me into Your presence regardless of how I mess up or how others see me. I'm so embarrassed at what has transpired. This situation seems to confirm all the worst things I fear about myself and has devastated me. I can't stop thinking about what others have said and how they've looked at me. The love and respect I long for seem lost to me. I don't know how I can keep going.

Thank You, Father, that You always accept me because of the blood of Jesus. Thank You for giving me my dignity and worth. This situation does not define me—You do. So please, Father, replace the feelings of shame and the condemnation from others with Your truth. You have adopted me as Your beloved child. You have created me, forming me for good works You have planned in advance for me to accomplish. You have indwelled and empowered me by Your Holy

Spirit, endowed me with every spiritual blessing, given me access to Your throne of grace, and called me to serve Your heavenly kingdom.

You have said,

> Do not fear, for I have redeemed you;
> I have called you by name; you are Mine!
> When you pass through the waters, I will be with you;
> And through the rivers, they will not overflow you.
> When you walk through the fire, you will not be scorched,
> Nor will the flame burn you.
> For I am the LORD your God,
> The Holy One of Israel, your Savior. (Isaiah 43:1–3)

Therefore, I don't need to be afraid. I don't need to isolate myself or go into hiding. I am Yours! You say I matter, and I will set my heart to believe You. Thank You for giving me the strength and courage to go on. Thank You for being with me through all this.

Forgive me, Father, for how I have believed otherwise. Reveal any way I have sinned against You so I can repent and walk in Your ways. Help me to forgive myself and others. You are so good to me, and You will empower me to keep going. You make all things new. So, Jesus, begin anew in me. Show me how to walk through this step-by-step. Give me courage and wisdom. Lead me, my Savior, because I trust in You.

In Jesus's name I pray. Amen.

WHEN YOU FEEL
Impatient

From days of old they have not heard or perceived by ear,
Nor has the eye seen a God besides You,
Who acts in behalf of the one who waits for Him.
—ISAIAH 64:4

Father, I confess that I feel edgy and restless about the situation before me. I long for answers. I yearn to see Your mighty hand intervene in this situation. Yet I know this is part of my training as Your disciple. David prayed, "How long, O LORD? Will You forget me forever? How long will You hide Your face from me?" (Psalm 13:1). The wait in David's life was an important part of Your preparation for him to take the throne, even if he did not realize it at the time. But You faithfully came through for him, and he was able to say, "I have trusted in Your lovingkindness; my heart shall rejoice in Your salvation. I will sing to the LORD, because He has dealt bountifully with me" (Psalm 13:5-6). And in faith, I will say so as well, Father—I will trust in You and will rejoice in Your goodness.

Father, help me wait with patience, wisdom, and hope. I realize that the more time that goes by and the greater the pressure, the more out of control I feel—and that is a great part of my anxiety. But time is a tool in Your hand, and You have a wisdom about it that is so far above and beyond my own. You see the end from the beginning, while I have only a limited view of the past and the moment I am in. Thank You for working on me during this time to stretch my faith and make

38

me more like Jesus. And thank You for orchestrating everything that concerns me in the unseen.

Lord, teach me what is important in Your sight. You see the future and what is truly vital for it. Help me to walk in Your timing and ways. Keep me from making wrong decisions, show me Your open doors of opportunity, remind me of what I need to do, eliminate wasteful and counterproductive time-eaters from my life, and help me remain patient and hopeful in the delays.

Likewise, Father, in these areas where I feel like I am running out of time, please lead me. You know how to make the most of every moment—to invest each one wisely in a manner that will honor You and bring peace to my soul. So teach me to number my days, hours, minutes, and seconds, that I may walk in Your will, be fruitful for Your name, and experience life at its best.

In Jesus's name I pray. Amen.

WHEN YOU FEEL
Inadequate

We are confident of all this because of our great trust in God through Christ. It is not that we think we are qualified to do any-thing on our own. Our qualification comes from God. He has enabled us to be ministers of his new covenant.

—2 CORINTHIANS 3:4–6 NLT

Father, I am so grateful that You are my God—my omnipotent King of Kings and sovereign ruler of all creation. Lord, the challenges before me seem so overwhelming because of my limitations, but I know they are nothing for You. You are God! You are the One who arranged the sun, moon, and stars in the heavens, gave Israel to the descendants of Abraham four times, and who knows my life from beginning to end. With the prophet Jeremiah, I say, "Nothing is too difficult for You" (Jeremiah 32:17).

I thank You, Father, for remembering that I am dust—weak and inadequate in so many ways. Ultimately, this is what causes me fear, dear Lord. I can't accomplish what I need to on my own. This desire in my heart requires Your supernatural intervention. Without You, I am without hope. But, Lord God, even in this, I thank and praise You because I know this need has come about in my life so You can reveal Your mighty power, protection, and provision. I know none of this is by mistake but is the perfect platform for demonstrating Your glory.

So I focus not on my weakness, Father, but on Your awesome strength. This challenge is not mine to overcome, but one through which You will reveal Your glory. I can't, but You can! When I am weak, You are mighty! Thank You for loving and providing for me. To You be all honor, glory, power, and praise now and forever.

In Jesus's name I pray. Amen.

WHEN YOU FEEL
Rejected

*He chose us in Him before the foundation of the world, that we
should be holy and without blame before Him in love, having
predestined us to adoption as sons by Jesus Christ to Himself,
according to the good pleasure of His will, to the praise of the
glory of His grace, by which He made us accepted in the Beloved.*
—EPHESIANS 1:4–6 NKJV

Father, thank You for accepting me. Thank You for always loving
me and never giving up on me, even when others do. Knowing You
will never leave or forsake me is a great comfort. Help this truth to
sink deep into my heart—the God of all creation loves me and sees my
worth. Thank You, dear Jesus, for saving me and making me worthy.

Lord, You know the rejection I've experienced throughout my life
that has wounded my heart, and You understand how deeply this
current situation devastates me. You see how worthless and helpless I
feel when others ignore me or cast me away. It is as if those who have
rejected me have confirmed my worst fears about myself—that I am
unlovable, damaged, unworthy. I call out these feelings, Father, bind-
ing and rejecting them in the name of Jesus because I know they don't
come from You and are contrary to the identity You have given me.

I recognize that many of these feelings took root in me long ago
and have a profound hold on me. But I am so grateful for how You
remind me of Your unconditional love and work to set me free from
these feelings, Lord Jesus. Thank You for healing my wounds and

42

giving me a sense of belonging in Your eternal, heavenly family as Your own beloved child. Thank You for blessing me with a sense of worthiness through Your death on the cross and resurrection. And thank You for filling me with a sense of competence and adequacy, empowering me to accomplish all You call me to through Your indwelling Holy Spirit.

Father, I must make a decision: either I will believe what others have spoken about me or I will trust what You say about my character and future. I know You are the only true and righteous Judge and that what You say stands firm through eternity, so I choose to listen to You, Lord. Help me to forgive those who have hurt me. I ask You to work in their hearts and heal the wounds that have caused them to treat me as they have. May it not be held against them. But may they know Your love and truth more deeply and be free.

Thank You for intentionally and lovingly planning who I would be and for knitting me together in my mother's womb with a good plan and purpose. How grateful I am for Your Holy Spirit and precious Word, which You use to liberate me from my pain and suffering. Thank You for loving me unconditionally. Help me to remember it is Your opinion that matters most—You give me my worth. Empower me to love whoever You send to me to care for. May everyone I meet see Your love and acceptance reflected through me. And may all people praise Your holy name.

In Jesus's name I pray. Amen.

WHEN YOU FEEL
Unloved

I am convinced that neither death, nor life, nor angels, nor principalities, nor things present, nor things to come, nor powers, nor height, nor depth, nor any other created thing, will be able to separate us from the love of God, which is in Christ Jesus our Lord.
—ROMANS 8:38–39

My loving, heavenly Father, I know You are good, kind, and compassionate. Thank You for caring for me, being my secure foundation, leading me in the way I should go, teaching me Your ways, forgiving my sins, freeing me from bondage, and giving me an eternal home in heaven with You. Truly, You have graciously given me far better than I deserve. Thank You for blessing me and making me worthy through Jesus. And thank You so much for loving me unconditionally.

Father, help me to feel and know Your love even right now. This sense of being unlovable has permeated my heart, and I can't shake free of it. I realize this is because of experiences I've had and lies that have been ingrained within me. So I open Your Word and ask You to lead me to Your truth. Remind me of how You carefully knit me together in my mother's womb, how Your eye has always been on my life, how You have drawn me to salvation, and the great price You paid for my redemption. Thank You for the great love You have shown me, Lord! I don't yet comprehend the breadth and length and height and depth of it. But what comfort it gives me to know that absolutely nothing can separate me from Your love.

Father, show me how to walk in a healthy, intimate relationship with You and with others. Reveal people You desire me to reach out to, and help me appreciate the people You have given to love me. And, Father, may my love for You increase daily.

I thank You, my Lord and my God, that neither death nor life, not my fears for today or my worries about tomorrow, nothing I can do or have failed to do, no power in the sky above or on earth or in all creation—not even all the forces of the Enemy—can separate me from Your love that You've given me through my wonderful Savior, Jesus. Help me always to walk in Your love and be Your ambassador of love to others.

In Jesus's name I pray. Amen.

WHEN YOU LACK
Self-Control

Everyone who competes in the games exercises self-control in all things. They then do it to receive a perishable wreath, but we an imperishable. Therefore I run in such a way, as not without aim; I box in such a way, as not beating the air; but I discipline my body and make it my slave, so that, after I have preached to others, I myself will not be disqualified.

—1 CORINTHIANS 9:25–27

Father, I am so grateful that I can approach You with any need. Thank You for freeing me from both the penalty and the power of sin. Thank You for showing me how to live in Your freedom. I confess I need Your help, Father. I want to live a healthy, godly life that honors and glorifies You. But I acknowledge that I lack self-control and that it is undermining what You desire me to become.

No matter how hard I try, Father, I can't stop myself. I do so much that sabotages my own progress. I have tried many times to find freedom in my own strength, but nothing I do helps. I realize I can't change these behavioral patterns on my own. They require Your supernatural intervention because they are ingrained in my flesh, and only You have the power and wisdom to set me free. So I submit myself to You, Jesus. I realize that so much of what hinders my progress is what goes on in my mind. A chain of thoughts ultimately reaps an action. And those actions eventually become habits. Like a rut dug deep in the ground, this becomes a pattern that once it begins is difficult to crawl out of.

Father, I confess my sin to You now. Please forgive me and show me how to fully repent—to turn from my ways of operating and follow Yours. Reveal where this issue originates in me, and root it out. I bring my thoughts and emotions captive to You, Lord Jesus. Make known the hidden triggers that send me off track, and replace them with Your truth. Give me the strength to fight temptation, leading me to verses in Scripture I can cling to in times of need. Help me to develop a biblical grid by which to examine my thoughts—whether they are from You, whether they are constructive or destructive, and whether they fit me as Your child. And, Father, when I am hungry, angry, lonely, or tired, remind me of how vulnerable I am and that I need to take shelter in You.

Jesus, I want You to be the priority of my life and the focus of my thoughts, because then not only will Your Holy Spirit empower me to have self-control, but I will have all that I need or desire in life. Thank You for setting me free from the patterns that lead me to sin. Thank You for teaching me how to live a godly life. And thank You, Lord Jesus, for never giving up on me, but always working to show me the way to victory. Truly, You are good, kind, loving, and deserving of all my worship and praise.

In Jesus's name I pray. Amen.

Section 2

PRAYERS FOR WHEN LIFE IS DIFFICULT

WHEN YOU ARE
Attacked

Hear my voice, O God, in my complaint;
Preserve my life from dread of the enemy. . . .
They devise injustices, saying,
"We are ready with a well-conceived plot";
For the inward thought and the heart of a man are deep.

But God will shoot at them with an arrow;
Suddenly they will be wounded.
So they will make him stumble;
Their own tongue is against them;
All who see them will shake the head.
Then all men will fear,
And they will declare the work of God,
And will consider what He has done.
The righteous man will be glad in the Lord *and will take refuge*
*   in Him;*
And all the upright in heart will glory.
                                      —PSALM 64:1, 6–10

Father, I come before You because of the onslaught that has come against me. Even before I begin, I ask You to shield my heart with Your forgiveness. Do not allow me to become bitter over this attack, because that would give the Enemy a foothold. I repent of any resentment that has already taken root. Rather, Father, help me keep my mind and my heart fixed firmly on You. You are my Shield and Defender. I affirm David's words: "In God I have put my trust; I shall not be afraid. What can mere man do to me?" (Psalm 56:4).

I praise You, Lord, because You see this situation in full—from beginning to end. You understand why this is happening and how I can overcome in Your wisdom, strength, and power. In Isaiah 54:17, You have promised, "'No weapon that is formed against you will prosper; and every tongue that accuses you in judgment you will condemn. This is the heritage of the servants of the LORD, and their vindication is from Me,' declares the LORD."

Therefore, Lord Jesus, I will follow Your example before Pontius Pilate and not say even a word against my enemies. I will not engage my opponents in public and will not attempt to do combat in my own strength. Guard my lips, Father. Instead of lashing out against my enemies, I will fill my mouth with praise to You, my great and mighty Defender. You are my Commander in Chief and my Redeemer. Thank You for working in the unseen to deliver me through this.

Search me and try me, Lord, that there would be no sinful way in me. Help me to repent and walk in Your ways in every area of my life. I set my heart to submit to Your direction and refuse to run even when everything seems lost. I will also see this battle as a tool You will use for some special blessing in my life. Indeed, I know that all the difficulties I face are ultimately opportunities that can bring me good and give You glory. So, Father, give me spiritual insight into the reason You have allowed this in my life, and help me learn whatever You are teaching me.

Thank You for giving me direction, strength, courage, and wisdom, Father. I worship You, my Rock, my Refuge, my Shield, and my salvation. Even when all my outward, earthly sources of security fail me, You never do. I know I am always victorious because of Your indwelling, enduring presence in my life.

In Jesus's name I pray. Amen.

WHEN YOU ARE
at a Crossroads

Who are those who fear the LORD?
He will show them the path they should choose.
—PSALM 25:12 NLT

Father, how grateful I am that if I acknowledge You in all my ways, You will keep my path straight. You know the road I am to take and what You desire for my future. I long to walk in the center of Your will and to make the decision before me with confidence. I want to be sure I am making the right choices, Jesus, so I need Your clear guidance. Thank You for promising that when I lack wisdom and ask You for direction, You give it generously and without reproach.

Lord, I acknowledge that I need Your help in making this decision. I am at a crossroads, and I don't know what to do. Each path has its challenges and its benefits. Each has aspects that frighten and dishearten me. I don't want to remain complacent or respond out of fear, Father. Rather, I want to obey You because I know You will lead me with wisdom in the path I should go.

So, Father, if there is any sin in me impeding this decision, I ask You to reveal it so I can confess it and repent. I realize that my personal desires and pressures from others have been getting in the way of this decision, so I bring them to the point of neutrality and listen to You. I affirm that I want what You desire. Your will be done in me, Lord. I also set my heart to wait for You as You show me what to do. Although there seems to be a time limit on this opportunity and pressure to proceed, I will not move until You show me clearly what Your path is. I will practice Psalm 62:1: "My soul waits in silence for God only; from Him is my salvation" because I know "none of those who wait for You will be ashamed" (Psalm 25:3). Lead me, Lord. I will not stop listening for Your guiding word. I will persist in prayer until You show me what to do.

Father, I ask You to speak powerfully through Scripture and give me promises I can cling to during this time. Give me promises as signposts to Your path. And, Lord God, speak Your peace to my heart as I continue to walk in Your will. May Your peace be the umpire that alerts me that I am safe and on track in this decision, my compass to assure me that I am moving in the right direction.

Father, I am so grateful that You love me enough that You didn't leave me here to make it on my own. Thank You, Jesus, because I know You understand how I feel, the inner turmoil of these choices and the aspects of this decision that fill me with fear. Thank You for sending the Holy Spirit to indwell me, giving me the ability to live in harmony with You and to know Your mind in any given situation. I bless You, praise You, worship You, adore You, and thank You for Your perfect guidance.

In Jesus's name I pray. Amen.

WHEN YOU ARE
Confused about God's Will

This book of the law shall not depart from your mouth, but you shall meditate on it day and night, so that you may be careful to do according to all that is written in it; for then you will make your way prosperous, and then you will have success. Have I not commanded you? Be strong and courageous! Do not tremble or be dismayed, for the LORD your God is with you wherever you go.

—JOSHUA 1:8–9

Father, how thankful I am that You are so ready to reveal Your wonderful plan for my life. I want to obey You, Lord. I want to know Your will and fulfill the good goals You've set before me. Thank You for loving me so much, for giving my life purpose, and for giving me Your Word to guide me.

Lord, I confess that I am confused about what You desire me to do. I am confident You will show me, Father, because that is what You have promised me in Scripture. So I continue to listen for Your direction with persistence and faith.

I praise You for this time of waiting—even though it is difficult—because it motivates me to seek You more and increases my sensitivity to Your presence. I realize that during this time You are revealing Your ways to me, helping me to know You better, conforming me to

Your wonderful character, and disciplining me so I can reach my full potential. Thank You, Father.

Please make knowing You and pursuing Your will the reason I get out of bed every morning and the focus of my life. With this in mind, I ask that You fill me with passion for Your Word, a longing to tarry with You in prayer, discernment of Your purpose in every circumstance, and wisdom in choosing godly counselors.

Father, please show me whether the desires of my heart are in keeping with Your plans for my life. If there is any way I am dishonoring You, violating Your Word, demonstrating a lack of wisdom, or behaving in a manner that doesn't fit who You are forming me to be, please reveal it so I can confess and repent. Keep me in the center of Your will. And as I follow You in obedience step-by-step, give me Your peace that transcends understanding and Your promises in Scripture to hold on to so I can know I am still on track.

Thank You for loving me and being with me, Lord. Thank You that there is no reason to fear or continue in confusion because I trust You are leading me to the best life has to offer. I have faith that You will show me the fullness of Your will in Your time. To You be all honor, glory, power, and praise in the seen and unseen and in what is known or unknown. You are faithful and true, and wherever You lead, I will go.

In Jesus's name I pray. Amen.

WHEN YOU ARE
Demoted

All of you, clothe yourselves with humility toward one another,
for God is opposed to the proud, but gives grace to the humble.
Therefore humble yourselves under the mighty hand of
God, that He may exalt you at the proper time, casting all your
anxiety on Him, because He cares for you.
—1 PETER 5:5–7

Lord God, understanding what has happened to me is difficult, and I need Your wisdom and grace in this situation because my
heart is burdened and broken. Whereas my life and plans should be
progressing, I have been demoted. I feel low, humiliated, and as if all
I have worked for has been torn from me and my road is at its end.

But, Father, how grateful I am that I still have the honor of
coming before Your throne of grace. I'm still covered by the blood of
Jesus, still Your child, and still have things You desire to accomplish
through me. You have not rejected me. You have good purposes for my
life. Nothing can take any of that away from me because it is You who
gave me life. Therefore, Father, I ask You to guide me in this season
of abasement. Help me understand what is going on, not just from
an earthly viewpoint but from Your heavenly perspective. You have
allowed this, so I know something good and important is in it, even
though at the moment it doesn't seem like it.

Father, my heart is open before You. See whether there is pride,
undue need for the good opinions and applause of others, a reliance on

my strength rather than Yours, or any other ungodly way. Identify and clean out anything that does not honor You or fit me as Your child. Show me where sin reigns in me so I can repent and follow You. In the moments that feel like there is no hope, remind me of who You are and how nothing can stand against Your ultimate plans for me.

When I have to face the people who have abased me, help me to walk in forgiveness and grace—both toward them and toward myself. Calm the fear in me. Extinguish the feelings of humiliation and regret. Remind me of my identity, worth, and competence in You. Help me put my heart into the work You give me to do. And in everything, show me how to exalt You in my words and deeds so that others may see You in me. Don't ever let me lose my witness out of hurt or bitterness.

I trust You in all this, Lord Jesus. I know this season is not for my destruction but so Your purposes can be accomplished. So lead me, Jesus. I humble myself before You and trust that this is not an end but a turn on my path that leads to greater things for Your glory.

In Jesus's name I pray. Amen.

WHEN YOU ARE
Persecuted for Your Faith

Love your enemies and pray for those who persecute you, so that you may be sons of your Father who is in heaven.

—MATTHEW 5:44–45

Jesus, thank You for being my Lord and Savior—for dying on the cross to give me freedom from sin and death. I love You and devote myself to You and to the proclamation of the gospel, regardless of the cost.

Lately, that has become costlier than I ever thought it would be. Protect my heart with Your forgiveness, Father. Help me not to grow bitter, and give me spiritual eyes to see through the attacks to what is really going on. I realize that those who are persecuting me are really responding to You. Your Holy Spirit is convicting them of sin, and they are lashing out because of the conviction, pain, and even fear they feel. What relief they would have if only they believed in the name of Jesus.

Therefore, Lord, I pray for those who do not know You—especially those who fear You so greatly that they consider You and Your people their enemies. Do not hold their sin against them, Father. Draw them powerfully to Yourself. Increase my love for them, and help me to tell them the truth of Your salvation, regardless of whether they persecute me or accuse me wrongly. I know I already belong to the kingdom of heaven and that they will perish if they do not accept the truth. Help me to stand strong for the sake of Your name and to be as loving and forgiving as You would be.

I trust You, Father. I have faith in Your protection, guidance, and wisdom. Help me follow in Your footsteps, as the disciples and prophets did before me. Prepare my persecutors' hearts for repentance, Lord, and give me Your words so that many can be brought to Your salvation. Thank You for hearing my prayers. I praise You that this is not an occasion for fear but an opportunity to bring in a plentiful harvest of souls.

In Jesus's name I pray. Amen.

WHEN YOU ARE
Stuck in a Bad Situation

The Everlasting God, the LORD, *the Creator of the ends of the earth*
Does not become weary or tired.
His understanding is inscrutable.
He gives strength to the weary,
And to him who lacks might He increases power.
Though youths grow weary and tired,
And vigorous young men stumble badly,
Yet those who wait for the LORD
Will gain new strength;
They will mount up with wings like eagles,
They will run and not get tired,
They will walk and not become weary.
—ISAIAH 40:28–31

Father, I praise You. You are the undeniable, everlasting, omnipotent, omniscient, omnipresent, and unconditionally loving God—the Lord, the Creator of the ends of the earth. You do not become tired or weary. Your understanding and wisdom are unfathomable. No obstacle is too difficult for You to overcome. Thank You, Father, that I can look to You for hope because the situation I am in is so disheartening. I am weary, Lord. I see no way out. And I feel as if the life has been sapped from me. But, Lord, I know Your plans are good,

You hear my prayers, You empower me to endure, and You make a way for me.

Father, I confess that I continue to be restless—I am still tempted to take matters into my own hands or settle for less than Your best. But, Lord God, I choose You. Right now, I affirm that I want You—Your will and Your ways—above all else. Please keep me on Your track for my life, in the center of Your perfect plans and purposes that You envisioned even before I existed. Help me to be kind and forgiving to those around me so I can be a good witness for You. Give me patience to await Your perfect plan. And prompt me to step out in faith when the moment is right.

Jesus, how grateful I am that as I wait upon You, You help me mount up with wings like eagles. You reveal Your will, fill me with Your supernatural energy and strength, answer my prayers in ways more wonderful than I can imagine, and fill me with an understanding of Your eternal purposes. Therefore, I thank You for this difficult situation and time of waiting. Thank You for all You've taught me and all You are teaching me still. I praise You for using this situation for Your good purposes—drawing me closer to You, refining my character, and preparing me for Your answer to my prayers.

Thank You, Lord, for redeeming this time, sustaining me when I am too weary to go on, renewing my strength, and fulfilling Your promises. I praise You, Father, for always giving me hope that the best is yet to come. To You, my precious Lord, I dedicate my life and all that is ahead. I wait in hope for You.

In Jesus's name I pray. Amen.

WHEN YOU DON'T
Know What to Do

*O Lord, the God of our fathers, are You not God in the heavens?
And are You not ruler over all the kingdoms of the nations?
Power and might are in Your hand so that no one can stand
against You.... We are powerless before this great multitude
who are coming against us; nor do we know what to do, but our
eyes are on You.*

—2 CHRONICLES 20:6, 12

Father, thank You for being my refuge, shelter, and help in every circumstance. I am grateful You have a full understanding of how complicated and confusing my situation is and how helpless I feel at this moment. I do not have the resources to meet this challenge, and I do not know what to do. The pressures are many, and the path is unclear, so I cry out to You, Father. I am so grateful that what I face is not a challenge for You—You are good, wise, and mighty to save. So I look to You for my deliverance.

Father, many people have opinions about what needs to happen, but I acknowledge that my comprehension of this situation is limited and inadequate. It is so easy to be weighed down in options and opportunities that I can't perceive how You desire me to proceed. Likewise, I do not fully grasp what You are accomplishing through these challenges. Therefore, only You can lead, Lord. Only You can decide what needs to occur because of the intricacies of the situation. So I will not be wise in my own eyes, Father, but will seek Your will and Your way.

I set my heart to pursue You and listen to Your voice, Lord Jesus. Bring me to the place that I can be neutral and hear what You are saying. I desire to do whatever You want me to do. Cleanse my life from anything that impedes me from doing Your will. Bring my heart to full surrender so that I can faithfully say yes to You in whatever You ask. I ask that You move mightily in the key moments of decision. Help me see Your will for every choice, and help me follow You in obedience every time.

Thank You, Lord Jesus, for making the way crystal clear. Thank You for protecting me and providing for me as I walk in Your will. I have nothing to fear, for You are with me every step of the way. To You be all the glory, honor, and praise. May everyone see and know that the victory in this is Yours and Yours alone.

In Jesus's name I pray. Amen.

WHEN YOU DON'T
Understand What You See

Then Elisha prayed and said, "O LORD, I pray, open his eyes that he may see." And the LORD opened the servant's eyes and he saw.
—2 KINGS 6:17

Father, I have observed some interactions and events recently that have put a question mark in my mind. I am not sure what they mean, and I do not want to draw any conclusions without Your guidance. So, Lord Jesus, I ask You to please give me Your perspective on this situation. Open my spiritual eyes and understanding to see Your truth.

I set my heart to be impartial and ask that You would lead me to answers in Your Word. And, Father, as You reveal more, show me how to respond or whether I need to do anything at all. I entrust all to You, with full faith that You will lead me. Thank You, Lord Jesus, for freely, willingly, and generously giving me Your wisdom.

In Jesus's name I pray. Amen.

WHEN YOU FACE
Spiritual Warfare

Be of sober spirit, be on the alert. Your adversary, the devil, prowls around like a roaring lion, seeking someone to devour. But resist him, firm in your faith, knowing that the same experiences of suffering are being accomplished by your brethren who are in the world. After you have suffered for a little while, the God of all grace, who called you to His eternal glory in Christ, will Himself perfect, confirm, strengthen and establish you. To Him be dominion forever and ever. Amen.

—1 PETER 5:8–11

Father, in this dark and fallen world, I know it is more important than ever for me to live as Your godly follower who is obedient to You and represents You well to others. Thank You for equipping and empowering me to do so. But I also realize that because I bear the name of Jesus, I will face opposition and spiritual warfare. Therefore, Father, I ask You to please make me aware of when the Enemy is attacking and help me to fight in Your strength, in Your way, and in a manner that honors You.

Father, prepare me for the conflicts I will face, including the one that assails me right now. Lord Jesus, I know the Enemy is active against me, because I feel tempted to sin and doubt Your Word. I grow disheartened at all the obstacles that have arisen against me as I strive to serve You. The Enemy is a deceiver, and he is an expert at making me think defeat is upon me. But I declare in agreement with the apostle

Paul, "Thanks be to God, who gives us the victory through our Lord Jesus Christ" (1 Corinthians 15:57). No matter how dire the situation appears, I know You continue to lead me to triumph.

Therefore, in the name of Jesus, I proclaim the victory is Yours, Lord God. I thank You for the armor You give me to stand firm against the schemes of the devil. I gird myself with Your truth, put on the breastplate of righteousness, ready my feet with the preparation of the gospel of peace, take up the shield of faith, put on the helmet of salvation, and yield the sword of the Spirit, which is Your Word, as a defensive weapon. Help me not to sin, Lord God. But if I should give in to temptation, convict me powerfully, and help me to repent quickly so that the Enemy will not get a foothold.

Father, I want to be strong and courageous. Help me face the battles before me with complete confidence that You will prevail over any opponent. I want to be Your effective servant in this world, and I know You can do great things in and through my life. So I submit myself to You for Your purposes.

Thank You, Lord, for giving me Your Holy Spirit to protect, equip, and empower me for whatever arises. Thank You for leading me. As David said,

> Even though I walk through the valley of the shadow
>   of death,
> I fear no evil, for You are with me;
> Your rod and Your staff, they comfort me.
> You prepare a table before me in the presence of my
>   enemies;
> You have anointed my head with oil;
> My cup overflows.
> Surely goodness and lovingkindness will follow me all the
>   days of my life,
> And I will dwell in the house of the LORD forever.
>   (Psalm 23:4–6)

Thank You for that assurance, my Lord and my God. I praise You that no matter the battle, I have hope because You are my Commander in Chief.

In Jesus's name I pray. Amen.

WHEN YOU FEEL
Everything's Against You

Do not fear, for I have redeemed you;
I have called you by name; you are Mine!
When you pass through the waters, I will be with you;
And through the rivers, they will not overflow you.
When you walk through the fire, you will not be scorched,
Nor will the flame burn you.
For I am the LORD your God,
The Holy One of Israel, your Savior.

—ISAIAH 43:1–3

Father, pressure has come from every direction in ways I never imagined possible. The odds are stacked against me, and I do not know what to do. It seems as if every form of earthly security has failed me. I have been disappointed by all of it. I call to You now, Lord Jesus, humbled by these circumstances and by my inability to help myself. Please forgive me for putting my trust in things other than You. You are all I have, Lord God. I see now that You are all I really need.

Father, I am grateful that You never abandon me but are always so faithful and kind, even when I do not deserve it. I think about how David said,

I waited patiently for the LORD;
And He inclined to me and heard my cry.
He brought me up out of the pit of destruction,

69

out of the miry clay,
And He set my feet upon a rock making my footsteps firm.
(Psalm 40:1–2)

That's how this situation feels, Father. Whenever I try to get a firm foothold, I sink deeper into the quicksand of trouble. But I know You can set my feet back on a firm place. I trust You will help me and fill my mouth with a hymn of praise to You.

Help me now, Lord God. As David did, I pray,

You, O Lord, will not withhold Your compassion from me;
Your lovingkindness and Your truth will continually
preserve me.
For evils beyond number have surrounded me;
My iniquities have overtaken me, so that I am not able to see;
They are more numerous than the hairs of my head,
And my heart has failed me.

Be pleased, O Lord, to deliver me;
Make haste, O Lord, to help me. (Psalm 40:11–13)

As David did, I turn to You, Lord. I recognize that my ways are defeating me but that You lead me to deliverance. Show me the sin in my heart so I can repent. Guide me on level ground so I can serve You. May this situation become a testimony of Your redeeming power and grace so that many will see, believe, and trust fully in You.

When I think back on all the times You have helped me, Lord God, I am so grateful for Your saving hand. I know You can do anything—nothing is impossible for You. You can redeem this situation and bring something good from it as You have done so often before. So save me, Lord. You are my Help and my Deliverer. I put my trust in You and praise Your holy name.

In Jesus's name I pray. Amen.

WHEN YOU HAVE A
Battle to Fight

There is no wisdom and no understanding
And no counsel against the LORD.
The horse is prepared for the day of battle,
But victory belongs to the LORD.
—PROVERBS 21:30–31

Father, how grateful I am for Your protection, guidance, and strength. Thank You for being my Commander in Chief. Truly, there is no Defender, Warrior, or King like You—in heaven or on earth. Regardless of the enemies or challenges in my path, You easily overcome them. No matter the conflicts and trials I face, You are always triumphant. I am grateful for Your love and guidance.

Lord, I recognize You observe the full battle before me and know exactly what to do. I also realize I perceive the conflict only in part—I see only what is immediately apparent. But You fight in ways that I can't even imagine, with both spiritual and physical armaments and strategies that are so much greater than my understanding or abilities. You are all-powerful and all-knowing, and everything is in Your presence. No one in heaven or on earth can help me more than You can. So I know I stand tallest and strongest when I am in submission to You. And I am safest as I walk in the center of Your will. Therefore, Father, You are my Leader, and I will follow You. I obey You, Lord, knowing there can be only one General deciding the battle plan.

Father, help me not to become angry or defensive at those who

71

attack, but to always be as forgiving and gracious as You are. Guard my lips, Lord. Help me always remember that so much of this battle is spiritual, and often people act as they do for reasons that are unknown even to themselves. My job is to obey You and represent You well. Thus, You call me to turn to You privately in prayer as conflicts arise—and not fight in public with words or actions. So that is what I will do, Father. Likewise, Lord, when I am hungry, angry, lonely, or tired, remind me of how vulnerable I am and that I need to take shelter in You. No matter what happens, I will not run away or give in to fear but will find my strength in You.

Thank You for always being available and leading me to success regardless of the battle. Thank You for working through Your Holy Spirit to guide me strategically around the Enemy's traps, to empower me for the struggle, to overcome every obstacle, to heal my battle wounds, and to direct me to victory. Thank You for revealing Yourself to me and to others through this. Help me to wait on Your perfect timing, trust You every step of the way, and be willing to obey all You ask. To You be all glory, honor, power, and praise in every triumph.

In Jesus's name I pray. Amen.

WHEN YOU HAVE A
Storm to Endure

He spoke and raised up a stormy wind,
Which lifted up the waves of the sea....
Then they cried to the LORD in their trouble,
And He brought them out of their distresses.
He caused the storm to be still,
So that the waves of the sea were hushed.
Then they were glad because they were quiet,
So He guided them to their desired haven.
Let them give thanks to the LORD for His lovingkindness,
And for His wonders to the sons of men!
—PSALM 107:25, 28–31

Father, I am so thankful that You are my God through darkness and light, adversity and blessing. You know all about this storm that has risen against me. None of it is a surprise to You, and for that, I am so thankful, because this is out of my control. Yet all heaven and earth are at Your command, my Lord and my God. So I call to You to help me through this tempest.

Jesus, I realize there are times You send storms for a specific purpose, as You did when You were with the disciples. You commanded them to go out to sea, even though, in Your perfect knowledge, You knew bad weather was ahead. Yet in this they saw their own lack of faith and how much they needed to trust You more. They had to experience You as the One who can command the wind and the waves.

73

I need that too, Lord. I must learn what it means that You are truly God in this situation and in every way.

Therefore, Father, I declare my confidence in You. I thank You for Your constant presence with me throughout the difficult seasons. You are my hope and my adequacy. I trust Your purposes—that through these squalls, You are preparing me for Your wonderful plans for my life. Thank You for perfecting my faith, making me a testimony of Your love and provision, influencing others through me, and teaching me to see my circumstances from Your perspective.

Father, help me to discern whether the negative thoughts I have are a spiritual attack, and lead me to verses in Your Word that I can call upon as a defense. I also pray that You will always help me to praise You—for rightly You are worthy of all honor and glory. Truly, it is good to give You thanks and declare Your loving-kindness. May I always be a faithful witness of Your unwavering goodness and grace, regardless of the weather.

Thank You, Lord, for being gracious and compassionate toward me and for taking care of me when I feel so weak and powerless. You have given me hope and purpose when they were lost to me. Thank You for helping me endure this dark and stormy chaos. Keep me on course in the perfect path of Your will so that I may soon walk in the sunlight of Your fulfilled promises.

In Jesus's name I pray. Amen.

WHEN YOU HAVE
Failed

My flesh and my heart may fail,
But God is the strength of my heart and my portion forever. . . .
The nearness of God is my good;
I have made the LORD GOD *my refuge,*
That I may tell of all Your works.

—PSALM 73:26, 28

Father, I come before You feeling so unworthy and despondent. I have failed. What I tried did not work. What I thought were strengths were revealed as my weaknesses. My efforts seemed for naught because no matter how hard I tried, I proved inadequate and did not succeed. I can't help but think of how humiliating it will be to see all the people who expected me to fall, reveling in my defeat. Of course, even that will not be as difficult as facing all who put their trust in me, knowing I've let them down. The worst part of all, Father, is realizing I represent You and have fallen far short of exalting You. May no one who serves You be ashamed on my account.

Lord, I do not know what to do. How grateful I am that You hear me when I feel so low and You continue to love me unconditionally. Thank You for not abandoning me. My impulse is to cry out, "Why me? What did I do to deserve this? Why did You allow me to get into this mess?" But I know this was my error, Father. So instead, I ask You to show me how I contributed to this defeat and what I can do to correct it. How can I get back in the center of Your will and obey You so You can redeem this situation?

Father, I want to hear what You have to say. I will set my heart to listen to You, knowing You can bring something positive out of this. You said in Your Word that You would supply all my needs according to Your riches in glory in Christ Jesus, and I need Your help in this struggle. Show me what isn't working, Father, so I can repent and walk in Your ways. Teach me how to rely more on Your strength and wisdom than my own, because I acknowledge I am not sufficient in myself.

Father, thank You for helping me courageously face all the people who celebrate my failure. Thank You for showing me how to make things right with those I've let down. And thank You for teaching me how to truly exalt You.

Thank You, Father, that none of this is wasted in Your economy. I completely surrender myself to You and look to You to bring good from this experience. I also thank You that my worth is not determined by this situation or any failure—past, present, or future. My identity is in You, Lord Jesus. And that makes me triumphant regardless of my circumstances. Help me to take hold of that truth in the deepest places of my heart. I praise You for always giving me hope and reminding me that the best is yet to come.

In Jesus's name I pray. Amen.

WHEN YOU HAVE
Sinned

*If we confess our sins, He is faithful and righteous to forgive us
our sins and to cleanse us from all unrighteousness.*
—1 JOHN 1:9

Father, forgive me. I acknowledge that I have sinned against You and violated Your holy law. I have specifically done so by [confess your transgression to God]. Thank You for Your Holy Spirit and for convicting me of what I have done wrong. I affirm that You are justified in what You have spoken about me. As David did, I ask, "Be gracious to me, O God, according to Your lovingkindness; according to the greatness of Your compassion blot out my transgressions" (Psalm 51:1).

Father, I know I have committed this sin for my own comfort, security, and pleasure. I also recognize that this evil has roots deep within me—that I have behavioral and thought patterns that make me fall to temptation. Therefore, Father, I ask that You teach me Your ways and help me walk in Your path. Root out the destructive lies I believe deep in my soul, heal the wounds, and retrain me to walk in a godly manner that honors You.

I repent, Father. I change from my direction to Yours. So as You address the wrong in me, I will obey You, even when I do not understand completely. Thank You for forgiving my sin, cleansing my heart, and conforming me to Your holy character. I worship You, my Lord and my God, and seek to honor You in all my ways.

In Jesus's name I pray. Amen.

WHEN YOU HAVE
Spiritual Strongholds

If the Son makes you free, you will be free indeed.
—JOHN 8:36

Father, I love and praise You. I am so grateful that I can depend on You wholeheartedly and for Your liberating work in my life. Thank You for identifying the idols and spiritual strongholds that have impeded my relationship with You and for helping me to be free of them. My hands and my heart are open to You, Lord Jesus.

Father, I confess the tension and frustration I feel in letting go of these unhealthy sources of security and worth. Please forgive me for trying to figure out my own solutions, attempting to "help" You speed up the process, being unwilling to surrender control, and for any way I have placed my desires above Your desires for me. Lord God, I want You to be first in my life and to trust You completely with my future. I want You to be on the throne of my heart. So, Father, please reveal whether I am harboring any additional idols and deliver me from them.

Lord, show me clearly which thoughts are causing me to stumble and how much of my time and energy I invest in deliberations and activities that do not honor You. Replace my erroneous beliefs with Your wonderful truth. Help me always to put You first and to arrange all other priorities in a way that pleases You. And, Lord God, please teach me to be disciplined about seeking You rather than clinging to anything else in the world.

I praise You, Father, because I know beyond a shadow of a doubt that You have my best interests in mind and that no matter what I release to You, You give me far better in return. Thank You for loving me.

In Jesus's name I pray. Amen.

WHEN YOU HURT
Financially

Do not be wise in your own eyes;
Fear the LORD and turn away from evil.
It will be healing to your body
And refreshment to your bones.
Honor the LORD from your wealth
And from the first of all your produce;
So your barns will be filled with plenty
And your vats will overflow with new wine.
My son, do not reject the discipline of the LORD
Or loathe His reproof,
For whom the LORD loves He reproves,
Even as a father corrects the son in whom he delights.
—PROVERBS 3:7–12

Lord God Almighty, I acknowledge You as my great Provider and Sustainer. Thank You for always giving me hope. This financial situation I am facing is overwhelming. I realize that as a believer, I should not put an overemphasis on money, because I serve You, Lord God, not mammon. But this situation makes me so anxious because of basic survival necessities, like food, medicine, and shelter. Not knowing how those needs will be met makes me fearful. How grateful I am that my life is in Your hands.

Lord, I know I have made financial mistakes and that I have not always honored You with my choices. Too often I have trusted in my own resources and possessions for security; and at times I have failed to ascribe all the blessings I have to You. Please forgive me, Father. I realize that everything I have is from You. Show me yet again that You alone are my refuge—the only One who truly provides for me.

Lord, You have all power to redeem me from this burden and indebtedness. Deliver me from this crisis, Lord God. Teach me how to walk in Your ways so this affliction does not destroy me, but rather becomes a testimony of Your mighty power to save. Show me how to transfer my dependence on earthly forms of wealth to You.

Father, I realize that depending on You begins by the act of faith of tithing. Forgive me for the times I have robbed You by not obeying this command to acknowledge that You are the source of all I have. Right now I claim Your promise: "Bring the whole tithe into the storehouse, so that there may be food in My house, and test Me now in this . . . if I will not open for you the windows of heaven and pour out for you a blessing until it overflows. Then I will rebuke the devourer for you, so that it will not destroy the fruits of the ground" (Malachi 3:10–11).

Lord, I take the step of faith and bring my offerings to Your altar in recognition that You are God. You do not need anything I have. But You ask me to bring it as an act of worship that grows my trust in You. This is my first step, Father. Help me to walk along Your path so I can be a good steward of all You have freely given and so I can find victory in this crisis.

Reveal Your glory so that all can see that from Your hand comes every good thing. Surely, Father, the person who trusts in You will never lack anything they truly require. Lead me, Lord Jesus; I trust in You. Thank You for helping me and providing for me. And thank You for hearing my prayer.

In Jesus's name I pray. Amen.

WHEN YOU LOSE
Someone Due to Conflict

Never pay back evil for evil to anyone. Respect what is right in the sight of all men. If possible, so far as it depends on you, be at peace with all men. Never take your own revenge, beloved, but leave room for the wrath of God, for it is written, "Vengeance is Mine, I will repay," says the Lord. "But if your enemy is hungry, feed him, and if he is thirsty, give him a drink; for in so doing you will heap burning coals on his head." Do not be overcome by evil, but overcome evil with good.

—ROMANS 12:17–21

Father, I have such a heavy heart today. No one likes conflict, but this one has separated loved ones—and that is particularly painful. Therefore, I ask for Your wisdom in how to handle it all. Father, please protect everyone in this situation from holding on to unforgiveness and bitterness. Do not let the bondage to shame or the temptation to blame others have a foothold in us. Show each of us where we have gone astray from Your path, and help us all to step back and consider whether this conflict is really worth losing important relationships. Lead us in Your truth, giving us spiritual eyes to understand what's really driving this disagreement, because we all need Your perspective and wisdom, Lord.

Father, I'm so grateful that I can turn to You in these times. I know

You care about these relationships and also the dynamics behind the disagreements. Certainly, I know I can learn a great deal from conflict—specifically, what my coping mechanisms, fears, and trigger points are and how I still fall short of Your image and character. You know each one's personality, strengths, and shortcomings, and You love each of us unconditionally no matter what. Help us to love each other as well. And show us how to stand up against the strain of conflict so that we may discover Your wise, healthy resolution to every problem.

Jesus, in Your prayer in John 17, You prayed that there would be unity among believers: "That they may be one, just as We are one; I in them and You in Me, that they may be perfected in unity, so that the world may know that You sent Me, and loved them, even as You have loved Me" (vv. 22–23). That is what You desire—that we would show we are disciples by the love we have for one another.

Help us not to lose our testimony or dishonor Your name, Jesus. I pray that under the leadership of Your Holy Spirit, Your people would "be kind to one another, tender-hearted, forgiving each other, just as God in Christ also has forgiven" us (Ephesians 4:32). That does not mean we must compromise on serious issues; rather, it means we should treat each other as You do—lovingly and with compassion, patience, gentleness, and self-control.

Therefore, Father, make me a peacemaker, after Your own heart. If there is a way to salvage these relationships, please show me how to do so. Thank You for being our peace and sufficiency in all things, Lord Jesus. Breathe harmony back into these relationships, and bind us all closer to You.

In Jesus's name I pray. Amen.

WHEN YOU LOSE
Someone You Care about to Death

We do not want you to be uninformed, brethren, about those who are asleep, so that you will not grieve as do the rest who have no hope. For if we believe that Jesus died and rose again, even so God will bring with Him those who have fallen asleep in Jesus. For this we say to you by the word of the Lord, that we who are alive and remain until the coming of the Lord, will not precede those who have fallen asleep.

—1 THESSALONIANS 4:13–15

Lord Jesus, I am having so much difficulty processing that my loved one is gone. I realize I do not grieve as one without hope. But at this moment, it's hard to believe life will ever be normal again, let alone peaceful or good. This separation changes so much. I am left with such a deep hole in my life, and I don't know how I will go on. It is so very painful.

Thank You, Lord Jesus, for promising, "Blessed are those who mourn, for they shall be comforted" (Matthew 5:4). I need Your consolation, loving presence, and peace. Thank You for not asking or expecting me to stifle these painful feelings, because that would only make matters worse. Rather, Lord, You teach me to grieve as You did at the tomb of Lazarus, over the city of Jerusalem, and as You prayed in the Garden of Gethsemane before Your death. Certainly, You understand how I feel and minister to me in my agony because You are "a man of sorrows and acquainted with grief" (Isaiah 53:3). You catch my tears and minister to my heart.

Lord, I am overwhelmed and weary in body, mind, soul, and spirit. Help me to lean on You, be patient with myself, and take things at a pace I can manage. Keep me from drowning out the pain in unhealthy ways, moving on too quickly, or expecting more from myself than I need to. I realize this is a time when I need to be especially careful when it comes to making big decisions. I also understand that there will be many stages of my grief as I assimilate this new reality without my loved one. Jesus, please help me not to give in to anger, guilt, bitterness, or despair. Show me how to accept this loss with Your grace and wisdom. I know if I walk with You step-by-step every day, I will get through this.

I also pray for others affected by this loss. I realize how difficult this is for them as well. Keep them from turning to destructive ways of soothing their pain; rather, may they cling to You in their grief. Likewise, help me not to be so consumed by my own sorrow that I fail to support them in theirs. Though the temptation may be to isolate myself from others, please give me the strength and wisdom to be present for them and minister to them with Your love.

Father, help me grieve with a sense of hope and purpose. Right now I am in agony and do not understand why such a loss has taken place. Help me face each day remembering that You too have walked through the valley of death. You too know what it feels like to be separated from a loved one. I thank You, Jesus, for never leaving or forsaking me. Thank You for loving me, answering the cries of my heart, and working Your divine purposes in this situation. Lord, even in this pain, You are good. Show me how to embrace my new reality with faith and to honor my loved one's memory in a manner that's pleasing to You. Take my heartache, and do a good work in me that I might glorify You.

In Jesus's name I pray. Amen.

WHEN YOU LOSE
Someone You Care about to Distance

God is my witness, how I long for you all with the affection of Christ Jesus. And this I pray, that your love may abound still more and more in real knowledge and all discernment, so that you may approve the things that are excellent, in order to be sincere and blameless until the day of Christ; having been filled with the fruit of righteousness which comes through Jesus Christ, to the glory and praise of God.

—PHILIPPIANS 1:8–11

Father, I thank You so much for my loved one, [name], and for Your plans for their life. How comforting it is to know that no matter how far apart we are, we are both still under Your watchful care. I pray You will give [name] mercy as they travel and in everything concerning this move. I also ask that as [name] settles into their new surroundings, that You will help them find everything they need. I pray this especially as [name] looks for a local group of believers to worship and fellowship with who will help them place their faith in You. May [name] thrive in their relationship with You. Give [name] joy and blessings in their new location, and may they shine brightly as a testimony of Your grace.

Father, please do not allow this distance to lessen or put strain on our relationship. I thank You for the technology that can help us keep in contact. But even more, I thank You for the Holy Spirit, who knits our spirits together in unity. Remind us to pray for, contact, and support one another. And as __[name]__ adjusts to the new locale or feels lonely, remind them that they have many who love them.

Thank You so much for the path You have for __[name]__ and all You have planned for them to accomplish. I look forward to all You will do through their life. May abundant blessing, protection, and provision be on their lives now and forevermore.

In Jesus's name I pray. Amen.

WHEN YOU LOSE SOMETHING
You've Worked For

Naked I came from my mother's womb,
And naked I shall return there.
The LORD gave and the LORD has taken away.
Blessed be the name of the LORD.
—JOB 1:21

Lord, how grateful I am that I can pour out my heart to You. I approach Your throne of grace confused and hurt. I know that nothing touches my life apart from what You allow. But this I truly do not understand because I believe You walked with me and directed me to achieve what is now lost. What makes matters worse is that it all seems so unfair.

So, Father, I place this situation on the altar before You. Protect me, Father—do not allow me to become bitter, and do not allow sin to have mastery over me. Help me to forgive those involved in this loss, and please give me grace for my own mistakes. I confess the pride of thinking I know best and I repent of it. You are God and I am not. You direct my life and work all things together for good.

Show me this loss from Your perspective, Lord Jesus—as a change in direction on the path rather than the end of the road. I praise You that Job, Joseph, Moses, David, and many more throughout Scripture experienced something similar, but You led them to greater blessings and usefulness than they could have ever imagined.

Therefore, as the apostle Paul said, "Forgetting what lies behind and reaching forward to what lies ahead, I press on toward the goal for the prize of the upward call of God in Christ Jesus" (Philippians 3:13–14). It is difficult, Father, but I let go. I realize this will be a process I have to repeat because this accomplishment was so personal—as if it were a part of me. But I set my heart to honor You. I know that in Your economy, nothing You begin is ever really lost but continues on until the day of redemption. You even promise to "restore . . . the years that the swarming locust has eaten" (Joel 2:25 NKJV)—so not even time is lost. The material parts of it may be gone, but the lessons, the growth, and the spiritual impact continue on—and no one can ever take that away. Thank You, Father.

I praise You, Lord God, that You are in all this and I can trust You. I praise You that in You there is always hope. Thank You my Lord and my Savior. Truly, You are good, and better days are ahead. I worship Your holy name.

In Jesus's name I pray. Amen.

WHEN YOU MUST LEAD
through a Difficult Situation

No man will be able to stand before you all the days of your life. Just as I have been with Moses, I will be with you; I will not fail you or forsake you. Be strong and courageous, for you shall give this people possession of the land which I swore to their fathers to give them. Only be strong and very courageous; be careful to do according to all the law which Moses My servant commanded you; do not turn from it to the right or to the left, so that you may have success wherever you go.

—JOSHUA 1:5–7

Jesus, I come before You today both as Your follower and as one whom others look to for leadership and as an example. You know the situation before us—how complicated, challenging, and even painful it will be. I place it on the altar before You. I know there will be difficult decisions to make in the days ahead, and I need Your wisdom and grace for that. Only You can lead us, Father, because only You see far enough ahead to know what is around each corner and how to successfully surmount each hurdle.

Lord, I confess I have not always represented You well before those You have given me to lead. Reveal the prideful ways in me and anything I have done that has dishonored You so I may confess and repent. How grateful I am for Your grace and that I can always come to Your throne with confidence. Thank You for always receiving me and often working good despite my shortcomings.

Show me what to do, Father. Lead me step-by-step. I think of the centurion who said, "Just say the word. . . . For I also am a man under authority, with soldiers under me; and I say to this one, 'Go!' and he goes, and to another, 'Come!' and he comes" (Matthew 8:8–9). Jesus, You marveled at that centurion's faith—and that's the kind of trust in You I want and need to have. So, Lord, be my Commander in Chief. Just say the word, Jesus. I want to confront every challenge and obstacle with Your wisdom and strength. As King Jehoshaphat did, I say, "We do not know what to do, but our eyes are on You" (2 Chronicles 20:12 AMP). And like Jehoshaphat, I trust I will see Your supernatural power and provision in this situation.

So, Jesus, I ask You please to make me a leader after Your own heart. Help me see what my people need and how best to guide them, even as I keep You ever before me. As adversarial situations arise, teach me how to be a peacemaker. Guard my heart against bitterness and unforgiveness, helping me always be a good example of Your love, wisdom, and grace. Lead me to make the sacrifices that need to be made without regret and to confidently take hold of all You have promised. Strengthen the chords that bind us together as a team. And may everyone who is watching this challenge unfold see You in a powerful way that draws them to love You more.

I know I have nothing to fear, because You are with me, Lord Jesus. I follow You. Just say the word and we will obey. To You be all the glory in this and every situation.

In Jesus's name I pray. Amen.

WHEN YOU MUST
Overcome Wounds from the Past

Behold, You desire truth in the innermost being,
And in the hidden part You will make me know wisdom.
Purify me with hyssop, and I shall be clean;
Wash me, and I shall be whiter than snow.

—PSALM 51:6–7

Father, thank You for beginning to show me all the ways that ingrained anxiety, hurt, and the Enemy's lies are undermining my life. I agree with You that my sinful ways, fears, and coping mechanisms do not achieve anything for me but more heartache. I realize that if I truly want healing, that my focus should be on You—my faithful, loving Savior, who sets me free by Your truth. Thank You, Lord, for working on me and releasing me from bondage.

Therefore, Father, I ask for You to do what only You can do in these places of woundedness. Root them out, Lord God. You alone know all the places where pain permeates my life and I lack peace and confidence. You alone understand why and how the concerns of life tear me apart. So I commit every aspect of my being to Your loving care.

Father, I confess that I've grown comfortable with my unhealthy coping mechanisms and I am afraid to step out in faith in obedience to You. But, Lord, I don't want to live this way anymore. I recognize that my anxieties keep me in bondage and prevent me from experiencing Your very best for my life.

Therefore, Father, please tear down the doubts that have become roadblocks to my faith. Show me how to root out the Enemy's lies and replace them with truth from Your Word. Wherever I am tempted to hide myself out of fear of failure, of being found unworthy, or of being judged as inadequate, please show me how to step out in faith and confidence in You. Reveal and replace the thoughts that confuse, trouble, and divide my mind. Expose the behavioral patterns that cause me to be destructive both in my relationships and my physical health, and mend what's been broken.

Lord Jesus, I commit myself to You, with full confidence that You lead me on the path of freedom and joy. Thank You for giving me the peace that passes understanding and restoring my soul. And thank You, Lord God, that even though You accept me just as I am, You care too much to leave me in a place that is less than Your best.

In Jesus's name I pray. Amen.

WHEN YOU NEED
Encouragement

This I recall to my mind,
Therefore I have hope.
The LORD's lovingkindnesses indeed never cease,
For His compassions never fail.
They are new every morning;
Great is Your faithfulness.
—LAMENTATIONS 3:21–23

Father, I feel discouraged. Sorrow wells up in me because of disappointments, losses, deep needs, and unmet expectations. Of course, You understand my sadness even more than I do. You see what is truly causing this deep hurt and making me feel hopeless. But, Lord, I realize that when I focus on what I don't have, my problems, or my regrets, they will always overwhelm me. They will always be bigger than they really are. So, Jesus, I will set my focus on You. Encourage and comfort me, my Lord and Savior.

I call Your faithfulness to mind, and therefore have hope. Thank You, Father, that You will always fulfill what You've promised. You have vowed to give me hope and a future. You have guaranteed that You will never leave or forsake me. You have assured me that You will walk with me on the mountains and in the valleys of life. I praise You because You are reliable, steadfast, unfailing, unwavering, constant, and trustworthy. You never forget, never falter, and You never fail. You are always unswervingly faithful in all things.

This is because You, Lord God, are omniscient—You know everything and, therefore, understand how to prepare, mature, and lead me in every changing season of life. You are omnipotent—You have the power to do anything and aren't hindered by any force on earth or in heaven. You are omnipresent—I am always within the reach of Your strong and loving hand. And You are unchanging—Your faithfulness endures forever. You can be trusted to keep Your promises in all things and at all times.

Surely, knowing You are with me encourages my heart and helps me to continue forward. You work all things together for my edification, and even the trials I experience are for my good and Your glory. Your precious Word gives me assurance, directs me through the changing seasons of life, and reminds me that no matter what I face, I can do so with absolute confidence. You have delivered me through many trials and will continue to do so. You have set me free from bondage and persistently work in me so I can walk in Your liberty. Your loving, faithful presence will be with me today and will accompany me in all my tomorrows.

There is no reason for my soul to be downcast, because I can put my hope in You—the King of Kings, Lord of Lords, my Great High Priest, Redeemer, Defender, and Provider. I praise You for how awesome, loving, and encouraging You are. Thank You for encouraging me and comforting me, Father. Thank You for forgiving my sins and teaching me to walk in Your truth. Thank You that nothing is impossible for You. Thank You for the precious promises You bring to mind and Your presence, Your power, Your compassion, and Your loving-kindness toward me. I will put all my hope in You.

In Jesus's name I pray. Amen.

WHEN YOU NEED
Help

Be gracious to me, O God, be gracious to me,
For my soul takes refuge in You;
And in the shadow of Your wings I will take refuge
Until destruction passes by.
I will cry to God Most High,
To God who accomplishes all things for me.
He will send from heaven and save me;
He reproaches him who tramples upon me.   *Selah.*
God will send forth His lovingkindness and His truth.

—PSALM 57:1–3

Father, I cry out to You in this hour of need. How grateful I am that You have not left me in this life to manage on my own. You are God Most High—my Refuge and Shelter, my Hiding Place, Rock, and Provider. Thank You for being not only my Savior but also my Lord, Deliverer, Counselor, Helper, and Friend. Thank You that Your Holy Spirit indwells me to provide all the wisdom, strength, and guidance I need, even at this moment when everything seems so dire. You are superior in knowledge, understanding, and power. Nothing I will ever face or require is beyond You.

I am so grateful for Your ability to deliver, Father, because this need is so far beyond what I am able to meet. But, Lord, I realize that when I am this unable to help myself, Your "power is perfected in weakness" (2 Corinthians 12:9) and You receive the greatest glory. So I cry out to You, Lord God. Be gracious to me because only Your super-natural provision can help me at this moment. I set my heart to obey You and submit to whatever You command because You are faithful to guide me through this trouble. I affirm that I believe You exist, are good and kind, and will certainly help me in this time of need.

I realize this situation is meant to teach me about You, Father. This is so impossible to me that it will show me that the Lord God truly lives and helps His people. So open my eyes to see Your hand at work, and do not allow me to remain the same. Turn me from whatever sinful way is in me, conform me to Your likeness, and help me walk in the center of Your will. Make this situation an enduring testimony of Your loving-kindness. May others hear of how You have helped me and trust in You.

In Jesus's name I pray. Amen.

WHEN YOU NEED
to Break Free from Bad Habits

It was for freedom that Christ set us free; therefore keep standing firm and do not be subject again to a yoke of slavery.
—GALATIANS 5:1

Father, I turn to You to break free from these bad habits and behaviors that keep me spiritually bound and in a state of defeat. As much as I have tried to find liberty on my own, I have been unable to do so. Please help me, Lord God. I know it is Your will that I live the abundant Christian life, and You've promised to help me take hold of it.

Father, I confess I have a problem in the area of [habit] and that I can't fix it on my own. I realize that this bad habit arose as a coping mechanism to combat situations that have made me feel insecure, fearful, and unworthy. So when I get right down to it, this destructive behavior is because of unbelief. I try to comfort and protect myself rather than trust You. So, Father, help me name these insecurities, fears, and issues of self-worth, and teach me how to seek Your answer for them. I repent of these damaging behavioral patterns and seek the fulfillment of these areas in You. Confront the lies that have been ingrained in me since childhood, and replace them with Your truth.

Father, I believe that the only thing that matters is what You say about me. I praise You for my position in Christ—which nothing in all creation can take away. I am redeemed, set free from sin, and have a new nature. I know You will lead me to freedom when I submit to You. Thank You for Your grace and mercy, Lord Jesus.

Lord, You've promised that You have a plan and a future for my life. Help me to know and love You more. Thank You for working to make me whole—emotionally, spiritually, physically, and relationally. You want me to be a complete person who is able to enjoy You, the relationships You bring into my life, and the blessings You have planned for me. Thank You for showing me where I have gone wrong and how to walk in Your path. Thank You for setting me free. And thank You, Lord God, for never giving up on me. I praise You, my Savior, and always look to You with hope.

In Jesus's name I pray. Amen.

WHEN YOU NEED
Wisdom

If any of you lacks wisdom, let him ask of God, who gives to all generously and without reproach, and it will be given to him.
—JAMES 1:5

Lord God, thank You so much for always being with me—for never leaving or abandoning me, regardless of what happens. I realize what a privilege it is that You've invited me to Your throne of grace, that I might receive mercy and find grace to help in my time of need.

I need Your wisdom, Father. You know my dilemma and my limitations in it better than I do. Thank You not only for promising to guide me but for doing so generously. How glad I am that You instruct me in the way I should go and that You counsel me with Your eye upon me.

I am so grateful that You will lead me through this and make my path straight. Like a loving Father or a gentle Shepherd, You direct me with knowledge and insight. And while You are shedding light on the road before me, You also drive out the sin in me, healing my wounds, developing my gifts, building my character, and teaching me more about You. Thank You, Lord.

You encompass me as my perfect Protector and Provider—and no one can break through Your defenses. You guide me with Your hand on my shoulder and encircle me with Your own matchless presence. I thank You that the only way anything can get to me is if You allow it for my ultimate edification and benefit. What great tranquility that gives my heart—that all things will work together for my good!

You keep me secure in Your steadfast, unending, unshakable love. Thank You, Lord! There is no peace like the peace You give, Lord Jesus! So I give this all to You, set my heart to want Your will alone, and await Your perfect instruction. Thank You for opening Your Word to me and showing me what to do.

In Jesus's name I pray. Amen.

WHEN YOU SEE
No Hope

My soul, wait in silence for God only,
For my hope is from Him.
He only is my rock and my salvation,
My stronghold; I shall not be shaken.
On God my salvation and my glory rest;
The rock of my strength, my refuge is in God.
Trust in Him at all times, O people;
Pour out your heart before Him;
God is a refuge for us.   *Selah.*

—PSALM 62:5–8

Father, how grateful I am that I can wait upon You and know for certain I will not be put to shame. Right now, as I look at my situation, I do not see any hope on the horizon. Every earthly answer has failed, and I can't figure out what to do. I realize disappointments are inevitable, but discouragement is a choice. So even though I am tempted to despair, I will put my confidence in You. I know You work to help me in the unseen and that You promise to prepare the way before me. Thank You, Father, that I can always hope in You.

When my heart wavers, Lord, please remind me to direct my focus to You. You are omniscient—knowing and understanding what I have never even imagined. You are omnipresent—going where I can't go and orchestrating solutions I don't even realize exist. You are omnipotent—accomplishing all I am powerless to achieve. And You are loving—always providing what is most beneficial for me. Even when You direct me away from something I think I want desperately, I thank You, knowing You are protecting me and leading me to an even greater blessing.

Lord, You are God! You are the sovereign, everlasting King of Kings and Lord of Lords. And You love me. I have no reason to fear, no matter how long I have to wait or how many obstacles are in my path. You will not fail or forsake me. And just as You formed the earth, sun, moon, and stars, You will form a solution for the deepest yearnings of my heart. Thank You, Father. I can always count on You!

In Jesus's name I pray. Amen.

WHEN YOUR FAITH
Wavers Because God's Promises Delay

The vision is yet for the appointed time;
It hastens toward the goal and it will not fail.
Though it tarries, wait for it;
For it will certainly come, it will not delay.

—HABAKKUK 2:3

Father, I praise You for the precious and magnificent promises You give me in Your Word. Truly, You are good and tenderhearted to those who seek You and comfort those who wait for You. Lord, I confess that as I wait day after day for the promises You've made me, I grow weary and my faith has begun to waver. Father, I believe You exist and that You reward those who earnestly seek You. But the pressure has increased, and the circumstances have gotten worse. It is becoming more difficult to control my feelings. I just can't see how You are working all this out, and I wonder if I heard You wrong.

Father, please confirm Your promises to me. I want to trust You wholeheartedly—with a strong, vibrant, and unshakable faith. You have kept Your Word and fulfilled Your promises throughout history, and I know You will for me as well. I realize my qualms are because of my own weak and vacillating faith. So, Father, I ask You to please reveal where these doubts are coming from and to heal me. Teach me to be patient and wise, steadfastly remaining on the path You've set for me, regardless of how long it takes or the obstacles I encounter. Keep me in the center of Your will, obediently following and honoring You even when I do not see the way ahead. I put my hope in You, my Lord and my Savior. You are powerful, wise, true, trustworthy, and reliable.

Thank You for revealing Your will and for always helping me to endure. Teach me to actively claim Your promises and obey You step-by-step in this season of delay. Lord, I want You to rule my heart and to be the focus of my life. I long to find my joy in You. I yearn to spend time worshiping in Your wonderful presence—with a passion for Your Word and a heart for prayer. You are my strength, comfort, and hope in times of adversity. You are the source of my life, my delight, my peace, and my all. I choose to obey You regardless of the consequences, because all my confidence is in You.

Thank You for drawing me closer to You, for working in the unseen on my behalf, and for preparing blessings that are infinitely beyond my best dreams, highest aspirations, and dearest desires. I trust You with every detail of my life and make You my first priority. I wait in hope for You, Lord, and know I will see Your hand work powerfully in my situation.

In Jesus's name I pray. Amen.

WHEN A LOVED ONE
Fails You

*At my first defense no one supported me, but all deserted me;
may it not be counted against them. But the Lord stood with
me and strengthened me, so that through me the proclamation
might be fully accomplished.*

—2 TIMOTHY 4:16–17

Father, I come to You with a heavy heart. In this time of trouble, when I need my loved one the most, it seems like they are far from me. I feel betrayed and abandoned. In this, Lord, I ask You to give me understanding and grace for them. I know they care about me in their own way but do not comprehend the struggles I am facing and have challenges of their own. But their lack of support feels devastating right now, Father.

Help me not to focus on how much I have done for them, their shortcomings, or how they may even be making this situation worse. That does not glorify You or help me at all. So, Father, please fill my heart with forgiveness. I rejoice that this is an opportunity to walk through this difficulty with You and to grow in faith and character. The truth is, I am limited as well—I need to learn how to be more sensitive and caring toward people when they endure the storms of life. Please show me the ways I have responded wrongly toward others so I can repent and make it right.

Thank You for never letting me down, Lord Jesus. You are always with me. You sustain me and give me Your wisdom and strength.

You comfort me with Your presence. Even when no one else understands what I am going through, Lord Jesus, You do—in a more profound and all-encompassing manner than any other person possibly could.

Therefore, Lord Jesus, I will fix my eyes on You and obey. Lead me to victory. Help me to triumph by loving those around me, being there for them, and showing them that You are my Rock and Refuge. I will trust in You, Lord. Thank You for always remaining faithful. I praise You because You never leave me or forsake me but are always with me regardless of what challenge I face.

In Jesus's name I pray. Amen.

WHEN A LOVED ONE
Has a Chronic Illness

Blessed be the God and Father of our Lord Jesus Christ, the Father of mercies and God of all comfort, who comforts us in all our affliction so that we will be able to comfort those who are in any affliction with the comfort with which we ourselves are comforted by God.

—2 CORINTHIANS 1:3–4

Father, how grateful I am that I can approach Your throne of grace for Your mercy, help, and understanding. I come before You today because of the condition my loved one, [name], must carry for the rest of their life. It is so difficult to watch them come to grips with this diagnosis, realizing that the pain [name] feels and the limitations of this ailment will never leave them—only get worse as time passes. My heart is broken for them.

Father, first I ask for healing on behalf of [name]. I know miraculously restoring them to full health is not beyond the scope of Your ability. Your arm is strong enough to save. I also acknowledge that You are the One who inspires doctors and researchers and can show them how to battle this condition. Thank You for the treatments You will invent through them. I pray You would provide one that will help [name].

I trust if it is Your will to glorify Yourself through this illness in this manner—through complete healing—You will do it. And all glory, honor, power, and praise will be Yours in abundance, Lord. But if You should choose not to heal but rather to give us the wisdom, strength, and love to endure this, then all the glory, honor, power, and praise will still be Yours. I declare that I will trust You whatever You may choose.

What I do ask on behalf of [name], regardless of what You choose to do, is that You will make Yourself known to them in a special way. Comfort [name] when despair, fear, anger, or helplessness sets in. Help [name] maintain their hope, wisdom, dignity, personhood, and identity as Your child, regardless of what may come.

Lord, I also ask for patience for all [name]'s caregivers. This is not an easy condition, and often [name] may unconsciously react out of pain, frustration, a lack of control, or a plethora of other feelings. Give their caregivers understanding, forbearance, and grace. And when we do lash out because of weariness or frustration, help us forgive ourselves and make things right.

Jesus, I confess that I do not understand all this. I don't know why You have allowed this or why You have chosen [name]—and by proxy all [name]'s loved ones—to endure it. What I do know is that You are loving and kind. You allow nothing to touch our lives without some good reason. And I need You to help me and [name]. So I will trust You, Jesus. As long as You have this for us, step-by-step I will place my faith in You. Be our strength and hope.

In Jesus's name I pray. Amen.

WHEN A LOVED ONE
Is Dying

*We know that if the earthly tent which is our house is torn down,
we have a building from God, a house not made with hands,
eternal in the heavens. . . . Therefore we also have as our ambi-
tion, whether at home or absent, to be pleasing to Him.*

—2 CORINTHIANS 5:1, 9

Father, I find it so hard to wrap my mind around the reality that soon my loved one will no longer be with me. This is incredibly difficult news, and I find myself avoiding dealing with it. But I know I have to. I realize that if I don't face it, then I will lose valuable time with [name] and react out of repressed, unprocessed emotion. So, Lord Jesus, please help me. Please give me grace and wisdom in this painful situation.

Father, if there is any way to heal [name], I ask You for it now. I know that at times You choose to restore people—You even brought Lazarus back from the dead. So if it be Your will, please miraculously heal [name]. Certainly, the time is short, and the prognosis is dire, but even now, Your arm is still strong enough to save. Show the medical community Your power by doing what they cannot.

But, Lord Jesus, even if [name]'s course is set and You choose not to heal them in this life but do so in eternal life, I will trust You. I say this with a broken heart and with tears, Father. You know how difficult it will be to continue without them. You know their loss will profoundly impact many. But I also do not want my loved one to suffer. Father,

110

only You have the wisdom to decide this, and I am grateful You do so with mercy and grace for all involved.

Father, help us all to say what we need to say to [name], and help them do the same. Let no love be left unexpressed, no conflict left unresolved, no forgiveness left ungranted, and no encouragement or gratefulness be left unsaid. But most of all, let [name] draw closer to You. Comfort [name] when the realities set in. May Your peace rule their heart, and may they confirm and strengthen their relationship with You. Please ease their physical, mental, and emotional pain and allow [name] to maintain their hope, dignity, and identity as Your child in these last days.

Indeed, console us all, Father. We need Your strength and peace. Help us to keep our testimony during this difficult time, showing that we do not grieve without hope. Likewise, teach us how not to be so consumed by our own sorrows that we fail to support others in theirs. Indeed, we rest in the confidence that because our loved one believes in You, we will see them again. May others see that in us and believe in You.

In Jesus's name I pray. Amen.

Section 3

PRAYERS FOR WHEN OTHERS NEED HELP

TO ACCEPT JESUS AS
Savior

He ordered us to preach to the people, and solemnly to testify that this is the One who has been appointed by God as Judge of the living and the dead. Of Him all the prophets bear witness that through His name everyone who believes in Him receives forgiveness of sins.

—ACTS 10:42–43

Lord God, thank You so much for Your love and grace. I'm so grateful that You've saved me, Lord. Surely You are good to those who seek You. Father, I confess my heart is broken today for those who are lost and will perish without You. Many people today worship wealth, fame, and other earthly security, believing those are the ultimate shelter from problems or pain and the way to freedom. Oh, how wrong they are. How I wish they could understand the hope You offer. Yet they run after possessions and pleasures that will devastate rather than satisfy them.

Father, please help the lost to realize the end that awaits them if they stay on this path—that they will be cast down to destruction. Show them that they can't earn their way to salvation by their good works or philanthropy, money, or power. Help them comprehend that the only true hope is in You and the only true wealth is salvation through Jesus Christ. When their flesh and hearts fail, may they seek You as their strength and portion forever.

Do not allow them to perish, Father. Show them how good it is to trust You as their refuge. Speak through Your people. Help us to tell of Your wonderful works so that people all over the world can trust You as Lord and Savior and walk in Your ways.

Thank You for drawing the lost to salvation, sending workers to the harvest, and hearing my prayer.

In Jesus's name I pray. Amen.

TO BE EMPOWERED
to Serve God

We have not ceased to pray for you and to ask that you may be filled with the knowledge of His will in all spiritual wisdom and understanding, so that you will walk in a manner worthy of the Lord, to please Him in all respects, bearing fruit in every good work and increasing in the knowledge of God; strengthened with all power, according to His glorious might, for the attaining of all steadfastness and patience; joyously giving thanks to the Father, who has qualified us to share in the inheritance of the saints in Light.

—COLOSSIANS 1:9–12

Father, how grateful I am that I can talk to You about anything, including the needs of my family members, friends, coworkers, fellow believers, and acquaintances. I may not always be able to help them, but I am thankful that through prayer I can lift them up to You—and You can transform their lives in miraculous ways.

Today I pray specifically that [name] would be empowered to serve You. I have no doubt that You formed this precious individual with great purposes in mind. Therefore, Jesus, I pray that [name] will be filled with the knowledge of Your will and with spiritual wisdom and understanding. There is no better place for [name] to be than in the center of Your will—trusting You as their Savior, being transformed into Your image, and obeying all Your commands. No matter what decision [name] must make or what obstacle they must face, when they walk in Your will, they will take the best path possible for their life and will have everything necessary to succeed.

May the way [name] lives always honor and please You, Lord, and may their life produce every kind of good fruit. Empower [name] to serve You through Your Holy Spirit. Enable [name] to grow in wisdom, skill, and love for You as they grow to know You better and better. I pray that [name] will be strengthened with Your glorious power so they will have the endurance, patience, and faith they need as they wait for Your plans and purposes to take shape.

As Your ambassador, Jesus, may [name] feel the responsibility to represent You well to others in conversation, conduct, and character and to be a light to those around them. But also, Father, help [name] always to remember that it's not up to them to make a difference in others' lives—rather, it is You who make the eternal impact through them. With this in mind, Lord, teach [name] how to rely on You and be a good witness for You. Empower [name] to avoid temptation and remain strong in their faith in the face of adversity. And fill [name] with joy and gratefulness—with a heart of praise to You.

I give thanks to You, Father, for [name]'s life. Thank You for enabling [name] to share in the inheritance that belongs to Your people. And thank You, Father, that You know how to lead and mature [name] better than anyone in all creation. May [name] submit to You and give You all the glory in every circumstance.

In Jesus's name I pray. Amen.

TO BREAK FREE
from Spiritual Strongholds

The Lord's bond-servant must not be quarrelsome, but be kind to all, able to teach, patient when wronged, with gentleness correcting those who are in opposition, if perhaps God may grant them repentance leading to the knowledge of the truth, and they may come to their senses and escape from the snare of the devil, having been held captive by him to do his will.

—2 TIMOTHY 2:24–26

Father, today I pray for [name] because of the concern I feel regarding the spiritual bondage they are experiencing. I am so grateful that You know everything about [name] and how to set them free from everything that encumbers their life. Thank You for identifying the idols and spiritual strongholds that have impeded their relationship with You and for helping them to be free of them.

Father, convict [name] of their sin, the destructiveness of their behavioral and thought patterns, and how much better life is as You lead. May [name] be open and willing to receive Your guidance. May You be first in their life. I pray [name] will trust You completely with their future and invite You to take Your rightful place on the throne of their heart.

Lord, show [name] which thoughts cause them to stumble and how much of their time and energy they invest in deliberations and activities that do not honor You. Replace their erroneous beliefs with Your wonderful truth. Help [name] always to put You first and to arrange all other priorities in a way that pleases You. Please teach [name] to be disciplined about seeking You rather than clinging to anything else in the world.

Lord Jesus, please send [name] wise and loving believers to help and encourage them in overcoming these spiritual strongholds and idols. Likewise, please give me wisdom as I interact with them—not hindering but helping their progress. Please help [name]'s friends and family to be kind, wise in how we teach, and patient when wronged. May we gently correct [name] when they are in opposition to You. Help [name] come to the knowledge of the truth, to repent, and to do Your will.

I praise You, Father, because I know beyond a shadow of a doubt that You have [name]'s best interests in mind and that no matter what they release to You, You give them far better in return. Thank You for loving [name] unconditionally and having a wonderful plan for their life.

In Jesus's name I pray. Amen.

TO BREAK FREE
from Unforgiveness

Pursue peace with all men, and the sanctification without which no one will see the Lord. See to it that no one comes short of the grace of God; that no root of bitterness springing up causes trouble, and by it many be defiled.

—HEBREWS 12:14–15

Father, my spirit is burdened for [name] because they struggle with unforgiveness and don't realize they are only hurting themselves with it. Lord God, I am concerned because I know bitterness is so destructive. [name] 's unwillingness to forgive not only undermines their future but also affects their relationships and injures others. I want to see [name] thrive in their walk with You, not continue to suffer needlessly. Therefore, I ask for Your holy intervention in this matter.

Father, I know there are good reasons [name] feels hurt. So I ask You to help me to be sensitive to their wounds and work through me as an agent of peace and healing in their life. I acknowledge it is only You who can truly lead them to lay down the blame for their pain and ultimately restore what has been broken. Therefore, Father, please keep me from becoming overbearing, patronizing, or controlling when I have the opportunity to counsel them. I don't want to unwittingly wound them further by operating in my earthly understanding. Rather, give me Your wisdom about what to say, and allow Your Holy Spirit to speak the truth in love through me and others so [name] may let go and be healed.

Please convict [name] of this bitterness. Remind them daily of how much You have freely forgiven and that they are responsible to forgive as well. Do not allow resentment and anger to ruin their life; rather, teach [name] to accept full responsibility for their unforgiving spirit so they can heal, grow in faith, and ultimately enjoy all the blessings You have planned for them.

I thank You, Lord Jesus, for the unconditional love and amazing grace You have for [name] and for the awesome future You have planned for them. I am so grateful that in Your great wisdom, You know the perfect way to lead them to liberty. Thank You for showing [name] how to break free of unforgiveness and live a life worthy of Your name. Thank You for cleansing [name]'s heart, liberating them from bitterness, and restoring the relationships that they have damaged because of the woundedness in their heart. Thank You for not giving up on [name]. I know they are safe in Your hands.

In Jesus's name I pray. Amen.

TO GROW IN THEIR
Faith

For this reason I too, having heard of the faith in the Lord Jesus which exists among you and your love for all the saints, do not cease giving thanks for you, while making mention of you in my prayers; that the God of our Lord Jesus Christ, the Father of glory, may give to you a spirit of wisdom and of revelation in the knowledge of Him. I pray that the eyes of your heart may be enlightened, so that you will know what is the hope of His calling, what are the riches of the glory of His inheritance in the saints, and what is the surpassing greatness of His power toward us who believe.

—EPHESIANS 1:15-19

Lord Jesus, thank You for [name]'s faith in You and the salvation You have provided for them. How grateful I am that You have saved them and have a wonderful plan for their life. Lord God, please give [name] spiritual wisdom and insight so that they can grow even further in their knowledge of You. Flood their heart with light so that [name] can understand the confident hope You have given to Your people. Draw [name] to You in prayer, and give them understanding as they read Your Word.

Lord, I know Your purposes include [name] taking their place in the body of Christ according to the giftedness You have given them. Therefore, Father, I ask that You would reveal how You desire for [name] to serve You and increase their love for Your people everywhere.

Provide strong believers to help [name] grow in their giftedness, and remind me to pray for, edify, and encourage [name] always.

Lord, I also pray that [name] will understand the incredible greatness of Your power for us who believe in You. This is the same mighty power that raised You, Jesus, from the dead and seated You in the place of honor at God's right hand in the heavenly realms. I realize that [name] will learn this through the trials and challenges where they find themselves weak but experience how truly strong You are. Indeed, [name] has no reason to fear.

For You, Lord Jesus, are far above any ruler or authority or power or leader or anything else—not only in this world but also in the world to come. God the Father has put all things under Your authority, Lord Jesus, and has made You head over all things for the benefit of the church. I pray that [name] will learn this and make it the anchor of their soul. May [name] never grow disheartened in their brokenness, but always cling to You and experience You in greater measure every day.

Thank You for making [name] part of Your body and Your family. Thank You for Your glorious plans for their life. And thank You for growing [name]'s understanding and trust in Your power and wisdom. To You be all the honor, power, glory, and praise in [name]'s life and in the church.

In Jesus's name I pray. Amen.

TO HEAL FROM
Illness

Heal me, O LORD, and I will be healed;
Save me and I will be saved,
For You are my praise.
—JEREMIAH 17:14

Father, I praise You for Your wonderful patience, loving-kindness, and tender mercy. You care about each of Your children individually—personally, profoundly, and sacrificially. Thank You for taking account of every hair on [name]'s head and every cell in their body. Father, I pray for [name]'s healing from the ailment that is currently causing them so much pain and discomfort. Please do not allow this condition to advance further or become dangerous, Lord, but cleanse their body of it completely. And please give [name] comfort, patience, and grace in this situation.

Father, I know miraculously restoring [name] to full health is fully within Your ability. If it is Your will to glorify Yourself in this manner, we give You all the praise. I am also grateful that You often use doctors and nurses to cure what ails us. You are the One who inspires medical researchers to invent medications, vaccines, and therapies. And so if You should choose to heal [name] in that way, may all glory and honor be Yours in abundance.

Thank You for whatever treatment You send and for healing [name]. Please give us all patience, endurance, and sensitivity for this illness. Help us to learn whatever You desire to teach us through it. And whatever may come, Father, may we all glorify You in it.

In Jesus's name I pray. Amen.

TO KNOW THEY ARE
Loved

For this reason I bow my knees before the Father ... that He would grant you, according to the riches of His glory, to be strengthened with power through His Spirit in the inner man, so that Christ may dwell in your hearts through faith; and that you, being rooted and grounded in love, may be able to comprehend with all the saints what is the breadth and length and height and depth, and to know the love of Christ which surpasses knowledge.

—EPHESIANS 3:14, 16–19

Father, I pray for my loved one— [name] . Lord, I pray to You as their Creator to remind them of the grand plans You have for them. You formed all the heavens and earth in Your wisdom and power—and You love [name] without bound. I ask that from Your glorious, unlimited resources You will empower and encourage [name] with inner strength through Your Spirit. Jesus, continue to make Your home in [name] 's heart in increasing measure as they trust more in You.

May [name] 's roots grow down into Your eternal, everlasting, unconditional love, and may those roots keep them strong—especially as You remind them to meditate on Your Word day and night. Make them like that tree firmly planted by streams of water, which yields its fruit in its season and its leaf does not wither; and in whatever they do, they will prosper. May [name] always have the power to understand, as all God's people should, how wide, how long, how high, and how deep Your love is. May [name] experience Your love, dearest Jesus, though it is too great for any of us to understand fully. Then [name] will be made complete with all the fullness of life and power that comes from You, Lord God.

Now all glory to You, our Savior, Jesus. You are able, through Your mighty power at work within us, to accomplish infinitely more than we might ask or think. May [name] always be aware of this and always cling to You. In the church and through all generations forever and ever, may all glory be to You, our Savior, Redeemer, Protector, Provider, Lord, Defender, and Friend!

In Jesus's name I pray. Amen.

TO MAKE WISE
Decisions

God is my witness, how I long for you all with the affection of Christ Jesus. And this I pray, that your love may abound still more and more in real knowledge and all discernment, so that you may approve the things that are excellent, in order to be sincere and blameless until the day of Christ; having been filled with the fruit of righteousness which comes through Jesus Christ, to the glory and praise of God.

—PHILIPPIANS 1:8–11

Father, how grateful I am for __[name]__ as they seek Your will. You have formed Your child with Your great wisdom and purposes in mind. I pray for __[name]__ and this awesome adventure that You have planned for their life. Thank You that it is a good, acceptable, and perfect plan. Thank You that it is a plan that will ultimately conform them to Your image and character.

Father, I ask that You draw __[name]__ closer than they have ever been and that they would delight in walking with You and obeying You daily. Lord God, clear out anything that hinders __[name]__ from knowing You intimately and walking in Your wisdom. If something is impeding their relationship with You, I ask that You would convict them of it in a manner that would leave no doubt and would compel __[name]__ to repent. Help __[name]__ to hear You clearly and see Your awesome face.

Lord God, I do not know the burdens and challenges __[name]__ is facing. What I do know is the great love You have for them and that Your plan is life at its best. So please help [name] to make a wise decision that will align to Your plan. When [name] faces overwhelming obstacles and challenges, sustain them with Your mighty strength, provision, and power. When they face long delays, give them patience and fill them with assurance of Your promises. When Your child has disastrous setbacks, heartbreaking losses, or devastating failures, remind them that You are near to the brokenhearted and save those who are crushed in spirit. Give [name] confidence of Your presence and help them glorify You in every difficulty. And continually remind [name] of Your great love for them, while filling their heart with love for You.

Help [name] to know and do Your will, O God. No matter how difficult or costly Your commands, give them the wisdom, courage, strength, love, and desire to follow You in obedience. Empower [name] to serve You and others with love, joy, peace, patience, kindness, goodness, faithfulness, gentleness, and self-control. I know the plans You have for [name] are awesome. And I know nothing is more worth pursuing than Your face and Your purposes.

Thank You for hearing my prayer for [name]. To You be all the honor, glory, power, and praise forever, Lord Jesus.

In Jesus's name I pray. Amen.

TO REPENT OF
Their Sin

Repent and return, so that your sins may be wiped away, in order that times of refreshing may come from the presence of the Lord.

—ACTS 3:19

Father, I am so grateful that when I do not know how to address a situation, I can always have confidence that You do. Father, I pray for [name] and the issues they are dealing with right now. I am so concerned because of the trajectory their life has taken and the ungodly behaviors they have become bound to. I ask for Your intervening hand in this situation.

Lord, I know You love [name]. Thank You for the salvation You offer them and the watchfulness You have over their life. I ask You to convict [name] of the bondage to sin they have entered into and help them be free of it. Show [name] that there is a better way to have their deepest needs met—and that is through an intimate relationship with You.

I confess, Father, that I have gotten frustrated with [name] and can be angry, fearful, and even resentful over their behavior. But, Father, I know that what [name] needs from me is Your strength, wisdom, and unconditional love. This sin is due to woundedness and pain that [name] doesn't want to face, so they don't need any more condemnation than what they already feel within. Therefore, heal [name] and help me always to approach them with kindness, humility, sensitivity to their pain, and with the desire to restore them to fellowship. I can care for [name] without approving of the behaviors that are destroying them. Therefore, help me to address [name] in love and truth, doing and saying whatever You require of me so that they will repent. Show me how to encourage [name] to obey You, and make me an instrument of Your peace to them.

Thank You, Father, for working in [name]. Lead them to recognize their failure, help them acknowledge responsibility for their sin, and convict them so they can walk in Your will once again. Thank You for Your work in [name]'s life and that with You there is always hope for restoration.

In Jesus's name I pray. Amen.

TO SEPARATE FROM
Unwise Influences

Blessed is the man who does not walk in the counsel of the wicked,

Nor stand in the path of sinners,

Nor sit in the seat of scoffers!

But his delight is in the law of the LORD,

And in His law he meditates day and night.

He will be like a tree firmly planted by streams of water,

Which yields its fruit in its season

And its leaf does not wither;

And in whatever he does, he prospers.

—PSALM 1:1–3

Father, I pray with concern for [name] today because of the company they are keeping and the activities they have been engaging in. Thank You, Lord Jesus, for saving [name], for the plans You have for their life, and for Your Holy Spirit, who indwells them. I am so grateful that Your hand is on their life. You see the friends and associates [name] has been spending time with and see the influence they have on them. Therefore, I seek Your wisdom and help in this situation.

Father, I pray for [name]'s witness. I know relationships go two ways and You can reveal Yourself to [name's new friends] through them. May the friends [name] has made all know You as Lord and Savior and grow in faith because of [name]'s testimony.

That said, Father, I pray for Your protection over [name] and even for You to separate them from these relationships if they are leading them away from You. Convict [name] of how they are drifting from You and turning to ungodly behaviors to fill their needs. Whatever desires these friendships are filling, Father—whether they be for acceptance, worth, status, power, or whatever they might be—show [name] that what the world offers is a mirage and only You can truly satisfy the yearnings of their heart.

Father, [name]'s life is in Your hands. Give me wisdom about what to say and how to continue praying for [name]. But I also ask that You speak straight to [name], showing them where these relationships are taking them and how they are undermining their future. May [name] be like that tree planted by streams of living water—finding their guidance, security, and worth in You. Thank You for loving [name] and counseling them through Your Word and the presence of Your Holy Spirit.

In Jesus's name I pray. Amen.

FOR THOSE SERVING
in Church

Obey your leaders and submit to them, for they keep watch over your souls as those who will give an account. Let them do this with joy and not with grief, for this would be unprofitable for you.

> *Pray for us, for we are sure that we have a good conscience, desiring to conduct ourselves honorably in all things.*

—HEBREWS 13:17–18

Father, thank You for the men and women who serve You in ministry and teach us Your Word. Lord, I know the work they do is difficult for many reasons. Not only must they endure spiritual warfare, but the burdens of tending to the needs of the congregation, crafting messages to disciple growing believers, and dealing with conflict are compounded by their concern to reach those who do not know You as Savior. Therefore, Father, I ask You to protect, provide for, and bless those who minister to us—and their families—in a special way.

First, I pray that You would open doors of opportunity for our pastors and ministry leaders to reach people with the gospel. Give them boldness to proclaim Your Word and serve You with courage. Empower them to wholeheartedly pursue the vision You have for their lives and for the church, resisting any pressure to stray from Your will—no matter where it comes from. May they reject all counsel that violates Your Word and always trust You to lead them in the right direction. I pray they can clearly, passionately, and effectively articulate the vision You give them. May they strive to be godly examples to their families, congregation, and the community and proactively grow others to be strong leaders as well.

Jesus, I also ask that our pastors and ministry leaders can find their identity and worth in You rather than in the approval of others. You have created and gifted each one so differently for Your purposes. In this age of competition, where the temptation is to compare the growth of their church with that of other churches or their popularity with that of others, I pray they can keep their focus on serving You in the way You created them to. Continually convict them of their inadequacy for the task and their need to pray for Your wisdom, direction, strength, and courage. Give them the joy that comes from living in the power of Your Holy Spirit. And encourage them, Father, through Scripture, time in Your presence, and in fellowship with other believers. Do not allow them to despair or fall to the pressure, traps, attacks, or temptations of the Enemy. Rather, help them to endure and be triumphant in You.

Help our pastors and ministry leaders keep their hearts and minds clear through a vibrant, growing, personal relationship with You, Lord Jesus. May they become even more passionate about prayer and Your Word—with contagious enthusiasm that spreads to the congregation and community as they faithfully proclaim the gospel with obedience, relevance, boldness, courage, and conviction. May they trust that You will take full responsibility for their needs—and those of their families—when they obey You.

I pray for harmony and a sweet spirit in the church—and especially among the church staff—as we all seek to do Your will as the body of Christ. And show us, Jesus, how we as church members can be a blessing to our pastors and ministry leaders and to their families. Give them grace, peace, encouragement, fulfillment, provision, protection, inspiration, and joy in abundance to the glory of Your name.

In Jesus's name I pray. Amen.

FOR THOSE SERVING
on the Mission Field

You will receive power when the Holy Spirit has come upon
you; and you shall be My witnesses both in Jerusalem, and in all
Judea and Samaria, and even to the remotest part of the earth.
—ACTS 1:8

Father, thank You for the men and women who have sacrificed so much to serve You as missionaries. I think about how difficult it must be for them, being so far from home, comforts, and support systems; having to learn new languages, customs, and cultures; facing pressure from communities where they are seen as strangers and intruders; and enduring spiritual warfare—all while fulfilling their calling of reaching the lost and discipling believers. Thank You, Father, for their faithfulness to serve You despite the challenges and for their part in spreading the gospel to the remotest part of the earth. I ask You to protect, provide for, and bless them and their families in abundance.

Open the hearts of the people they are ministering to, and supernaturally empower your servants to communicate to those around them in meaningful ways. Regardless of the pressure or persecution they encounter, give them boldness and courage in proclaiming Your Word, and let Your fruit of the Spirit flow through them as they interact with others. Please provide them with new believers whom they can disciple and raise up as strong, godly leaders for the church.

Bless the missionaries with resilient and faithful friendships, prayer warriors, and ministry partners who will give them unwavering support regardless of what they face. In their times of loneliness, sadness, trial, or disappointment, remind them to find their identity, hope, and worth in You. Help them to remember that You are the One who defines success and who works through them for Your will and pleasure. May they become even more passionate about prayer and Your Word—with contagious enthusiasm and godly conduct that inspires those they meet.

Encourage them, Father, through Scripture, time in Your presence, and in fellowship with other believers. Protect them from the pressure, traps, attacks, and temptations of the Enemy. Rather, help them to endure and be triumphant in You—with clean hearts and clear minds that come from a strong, growing, personal relationship with You. May they trust that You will take full responsibility for their needs—and those of their families—when they obey You.

Thank You, Father, for being with the missionaries. May they continue faithfully proclaiming the gospel with obedience, relevance, boldness, courage, and conviction regardless of what they face. May they always experience Your provision, protection, grace, peace, encouragement, fulfillment, and joy in abundance. And may they see You bring a great harvest from all the obedience they've sown, to the glory of Your name.

In Jesus's name I pray. Amen.

FOR THOSE SERVING
in Places Antagonistic to the Gospel

Blessed are those who have been persecuted for the sake of righteousness, for theirs is the kingdom of heaven.

Blessed are you when people insult you and persecute you, and falsely say all kinds of evil against you because of Me. Rejoice and be glad, for your reward in heaven is great; for in the same way they persecuted the prophets who were before you.

—MATTHEW 5:10–12

Father, I approach Your throne of grace for my brothers and sisters in Christ around the world who are being persecuted for their faith. They are being separated from their families, rejected, denied basic needs, beaten, thrown in jail, and even killed because they claim the name of Jesus. When I think of them, Lord God, I am humbled to consider their courage and commitment to You. I know You guide them with Your eye upon them, have numbered every hair on their heads, and catch their every tear. I am so grateful that You honor their testimony in a special way. Thank You for their witness in such dark and difficult places. Thank You for how You multiply their influence, provide for them, and comfort them. I ask You to protect them, supply their needs, and bless them in abundance.

I thank You, Father, that through Your remnant of faithful believers, Your good news of salvation is alive in these areas resistant to

Christianity. Make these persecuted Christians bright and powerful witnesses for the sake of Your name. Give them wisdom for when to speak with boldness and when to be silent—and the right words that will pierce to the hearts of those who hear them. I pray for their oppressors—that Your Holy Spirit would convict them of the truth, of the wrongs they have done, the emptiness of false religions, and of their need of salvation through Jesus. Make Your hope, forgiveness, perseverance, and fruit of the Spirit flow through the persecuted Christians so they can maintain their testimony toward those who torment them. I pray this especially for the believers who are rejected by family and friends. Father, may other believers arise, surround them as a new Christian family, and support them.

I praise You that persecuted believers can always seek You as their hope and peace, regardless of what happens. You are their strength and sufficiency, Lord God. Sustain them. Make Your loving presence known to them in a powerful way. Give them spiritual eyes to understand the warfare that comes against them from the forces of darkness. Help them to endure and be triumphant in You—with the clean hearts and clear minds that come from a strong, growing, personal relationship with You. If they do not have a Bible, please provide them one, Father. Give them Your insight and teach them Your truth, and may they experience the blessing of worshiping You, maturing in You, and fellowshiping with other believers. May they trust that You will take full responsibility for their needs as they obey You. And may they see Your powerful hand intervening supernaturally in their situations.

Finally, I pray that You would stir the church around the world to take a stand for our persecuted brothers and sisters in the faith. Let us not become complacent or entitled, Father, but burden our hearts for other Christians throughout the world who are suffering. Also, Father, I pray that You would move world leaders to stop the inhumane maltreatment and oppression of Christians. Give me a heart like those of my persecuted brothers and sisters—proclaiming the truth with boldness despite the pressure—and show me how I can be a blessing to them.

Thank You for their example and testimony. Thank You, Father, for taking care of them and showing Yourself powerful on their behalf. And thank You, Lord, that they will see a great harvest from all the obedience they've sown, to the glory of Your name.

In Jesus's name I pray. Amen.

FOR THOSE SERVING
as Leaders

*I urge that entreaties and prayers, petitions and thanksgivings,
be made on behalf of all men, for kings and all who are in
authority, so that we may lead a tranquil and quiet life in all
godliness and dignity. This is good and acceptable in the sight of
God our Savior, who desires all men to be saved and to come to
the knowledge of the truth.*

—1 TIMOTHY 2:1–4

Father, thank You for loving and protecting Your people. I know,
Lord, that You raise up leaders and remove them for Your purposes
and that their hearts are in Your hands and that You can work
through anyone. You also command me to pray for these leaders—that
they would turn to You and serve You. Therefore, Father, I pray for
those who serve as our leaders—that they would seek You and submit
themselves to You. I realize that not all our leaders acknowledge You
and that there are those who would lead us away from Your best. But
I am thankful that You know them by name and love them. Father,
take hold of them and lead them to do Your will.

Lord, I pray You will cause people in authority to realize their sin-
fulness and daily need for Your forgiveness and guidance. If they do
not know Jesus as their Savior, I ask that You draw them to Yourself,
convict them of their sins, and bring them to salvation. Please help
them to admit their personal inadequacies for the tasks ahead and
to turn to You for the wisdom, discernment, and courage to carry out

their responsibilities. I pray they will reject all counsel that violates the spiritual principles set forth in Scripture and that they will trust You to lead them in the best direction. May they be able to resist pressure from those who would lead them astray or tempt them to violate Your will and the clear standards of right and wrong.

Father, I pray that those in authority will actively work to reverse the trends that dethrone You and deify man. May they be willing to abandon their personal ambitions if doing so is in the best interests of the people they lead. May they rely upon prayer, the truth of Your Word, and the direction of Your Holy Spirit for their daily strength and path to success. And, Father, may our leaders restore dignity, honor, trustworthiness, and righteousness to their offices. May they strive to be good examples to the people—especially the children—in our nation, remembering daily that they are accountable to You, Almighty God, for their attitudes, words, motives, and actions.

Thank You for being our righteous Judge and King. We praise You for hearing our prayers and that "the king's heart is like channels of water in the hand of the LORD" (Proverbs 21:1). Direct us all in the way we should go.

In Jesus's name I pray. Amen.

FOR THOSE SERVING
in the Military

Because he has loved Me, therefore I will deliver him;
I will set him securely on high, because he has known My name.
He will call upon Me, and I will answer him;
I will be with him in trouble;
I will rescue him and honor him.

—PSALM 91:14–15

Father, today I pray for [name], who is serving in the military. I pray that they would live in Your shelter, Most High God. Help them find rest in You, Almighty God. This I declare about You, Lord—You are the only true refuge and place of safety. You are my God, and I have faith in You. I pray [name] will fully trust in You as well and be Your representative to their fellow soldiers. Be their peace and place of security always. Rescue them from every trap, and protect them from deadly disease and danger. Guard [name] with Your mighty arm.

Father, Your faithful promises are [name]'s armor and protection. May they not be afraid of the terrors of the night nor the armaments that fly in the daytime. Protect their fellow soldiers, and give the assurance that evil will not overcome them. Give wisdom to the commanders and all who make decisions. Open [name]'s eyes to those who desire to do evil, help them to see through their plots, and lead them to triumph. Help them to keep steady, give You all their anxieties, and take comfort in Your name. And may [name] be a faithful witness of Your grace, Lord Jesus, to whomever they may meet, whether friend or foe.

Thank You, Father, for ordering Your angels to protect [name] wherever they go. Thank You, Father, for trampling the Enemy under Your feet. Lord, You say,

> I will rescue those who love me.
>> I will protect those who trust in my name.
> When they call on me, I will answer;
>> I will be with them in trouble.
>> I will rescue and honor them.
> I will reward them with a long life
>> and give them my salvation. (Psalm 91:14–16 NLT)

Thank You for this promise for [name] and for all who serve You. In Jesus's name I pray. Amen.

WHEN A BABY
Is Born

You formed my inward parts;
You wove me in my mother's womb.
I will give thanks to You, for I am fearfully and wonderfully made;
Wonderful are Your works,
And my soul knows it very well.

—PSALM 139:13–14

Father, thank You for the new life of this precious child— [name] . Thank You for giving them life and for the good purposes for which You have created them. [name] is fearfully and wonderfully made because Your works, Father, are wonderful, and You make no mistakes. Thank You that they have been born to [parents' names] during this time in history, in this geographical location, with their particular personality, gifts, and talents to fulfill Your divine plans.

Lord, I pray that as [name] grows up, they will be influenced daily to walk in Your will and love You with their whole heart, mind, soul, and strength. I thank You in advance for the day [name] accepts You as Savior and Lord, committing their life to You wholeheartedly.

Father, help [name] number their days aright even from the beginning, and teach them wisdom deep within their heart. I pray for godly friends and even a godly mate to walk with [name] through their life. Lead them to make good choices.

Thank You for all You have planned in advance for [name] to do. However You choose to work through [name] , may they set their heart to glorify You in their conduct, character, and speech. And may many people know You as Savior because of [name] 's testimony of Your grace.

In Jesus's name I pray. Amen.

WHEN A BELIEVER
Is Baptized

Do you not know that all of us who have been baptized into
Christ Jesus have been baptized into His death? Therefore we
have been buried with Him through baptism into death, so
that as Christ was raised from the dead through the glory of the
Father, so we too might walk in newness of life.

—ROMANS 6:3–4

Father, how grateful I am for [name], who has taken the important step of baptism in obedience to You. Though baptism does not save us, it shows our willingness to publicly proclaim You as our Savior and Lord. Thank You for saving [name] and for their testimony today.

Lord, as [name] is immersed in the baptismal waters, help them fully understand that their old nature is gone and has been buried— just as Christ was. [name]'s baptism illustrates that when they accepted Jesus as Savior, their sin was removed from them "as far as the east is from the west" (Psalm 103:12), never to return again. Help [name] to understand this wonderful truth in their heart.

[name]'s baptism is also symbolic of the powerful resurrection life every believer has in Christ as a born again, spiritually alive, and Holy Spirit–empowered child of the Living God. So as [name] is raised from the baptismal waters, reveal the awesome new life they have been given, and help them take hold of it.

May this step of obedience be the first of many more for [name], as they find their place in the body of Christ. I thank You for all You have planned to accomplish through [name]. And may [name]'s life continue to be a testimony of Your glory and grace now and forevermore.

In Jesus's name I pray. Amen.

WHEN A STUDENT
Graduates

Do not call to mind the former things,
Or ponder things of the past.
Behold, I will do something new,
Now it will spring forth;
Will you not be aware of it?
I will even make a roadway in the wilderness,
Rivers in the desert.

—ISAIAH 43:18–19

Father, I thank You for [name] and for this achievement and milestone in their life. Graduation signifies a new beginning—a new step into a bright future. Thank You, Father, for the wonderful plan You have for [name]'s life. Thank You for bringing them this far and that You will be with them in all their tomorrows.

Father, in the weeks and months to come, [name] will be making decisions that will affect the course of their future. Give [name] wisdom, and lead them in Your truth. Thank You, Father, that we know You can help [name] live a truly extraordinary life and that You will lead them on the best path possible as they obey You.

Father, I pray You would keep [name] from falling into the trap of placing their hope in temporal things—money, social status, achievements, or even the acceptance of others. Worldly comforts are no defense against the tumultuous storms that life often delivers.

Help [name] base their identity and worth on You so they can stand strong regardless of what tempest arises.

Give [name] a hunger for Your Word, and teach them Your principles for walking in Your success, hope, peace, and victory. May [name] know You and love You more daily. May they decrease as You sanctify them and shine through their life. Show [name] how beloved they are and how great Your calling is, Lord. May [name] eagerly desire to live for You and through Your power.

Thank You, Father, for working through [name], making them Your witness in the world, and forming them into Your masterpiece. May [name] walk in the extraordinary life You have planned for them.

In Jesus's name I pray. Amen.

WHEN TWO ARE
United in Marriage

A man shall leave his father and mother and be joined to his wife, and the two shall become one flesh. So they are no longer two, but one flesh. What therefore God has joined together, let no man separate.

—MATTHEW 19:5-6

Father, how grateful I am for [name] and [name] as they unite in marriage in Your name. I thank You for their commitment to You and to each other. I praise You for how You have created each of them with complementary gifts, personalities, and skills and have brought them together to serve You as one flesh.

Lord, as they begin their journey hand-in-hand, I ask that Your grace and their love for each other will increase in both the mountain-tops and valleys—in the blessings and in the difficulties of life. May they grow together even further through the good and bad, as they both fix their eyes on You.

I pray that [husband] will treasure, honor, and nurture [wife] as Christ loved the church—even giving Himself sacrificially for her. I also pray [wife] will cherish, respect, and care for [husband], likewise sacrificially, as the church should Christ. This is the manner by which unconditional love, holiness, respect, and relationships mature. And this is the manner by which [name] and [name] will find ultimate success in their marriage—to Your glory.

May neither seek their own interests but put each other's first.

May they be patient and kind toward one another, not being jealous, vengeful, bitter, or wise in their own eyes. Rather, may they always be gentle, humble, self-controlled, wise, and forgiving as they interact. May they give each other the grace and support to become all You created each of them to become and serve You in the manner You formed them to serve You. May they be better because they are together than they ever would have been apart. And, Father, when temptation and hurts arise, I pray You would act on their behalf and protect this covenant of matrimony. Let no man, adversity, or opportunity tear asunder what You have joined together.

Thank You, Father, for the future You have planned for [name] and [name]. To You be all the honor, glory, power, and praise in their union and forevermore.

In Jesus's name I pray. Amen.

WHEN NATIONAL
Tragedy Strikes

The LORD is my light and my salvation;
Whom shall I fear?
The LORD is the defense of my life;
Whom shall I dread? . . .
For in the day of trouble He will conceal me in His tabernacle;
In the secret place of His tent He will hide me;
He will lift me up on a rock.

—PSALM 27:1, 5

Father, how grateful I am that we can approach You in these times of devastation. You said You would listen to us when we cry out to you, so I beseech You on behalf of all the people who are hurting and those who feel lost, shaken, angry, and helpless. Father, when I consider the overwhelming loss, the suddenness of the destruction, and the separation of children from their parents, I am struck by the sense of hopelessness and confusion that people must feel. Lord God, in these moments, we all need You most and need to feel Your presence.

For those who do not know You, Lord, I ask that You would deliver the truth of the gospel to them through the believers around them and those whom You will send for relief. Lead Christians to them who will love them, encourage them, and help them emotionally, physically, and spiritually so that they will know that the message of salvation through Jesus Christ is true. For all involved, send the aid they need, to help them in whatever manner they require.

Thank You, Lord, for all the first responders and the brave people who sprang into action to help those who were hurting. We ask Your special blessing on their lives. May the church likewise come together in unity to shine the light of Your love and provision on this situation. Help us to be caring, sensitive, and sacrificial—and thereby glorify You.

Father, I know that evil is always present and that there are always people who will try to exploit such a crisis to advance their own agendas. Prevent them, Father. Do not allow them to take advantage of the innocent or to triumph in this. Instead, Lord, show Yourself in a mighty way. You are the only One greater than any tragedy, disaster, or evil force in this world. And You are the only One who offers us eternal life—and thereby, an everlasting hope. So comfort the afflicted, draw the lost to salvation, bring justice, and show mercy.

Thank You, Father, for being the refuge we can run to in such times. It is difficult to wrap our minds around the pictures we are seeing of this tragedy—never mind offer consolation, restoration, and healing to those affected by it. And yet You offer us comfort and peace in the midst of tragedy. Thank You for showing us that there is more to this life than heartbreak, loss, and disaster. Thank You for being our Protector and Provider and for giving us a home that awaits us in heaven, where there are no more tears, no more pain, no more evil, no more death, and where we will be reunited with our loved ones. Help us build our lives on the unshakable foundation of Your love and to be Your hands and feet to those who are hurting.

In Jesus's name I pray. Amen.

Section 4

PRAYERS FOR WHEN YOU FEEL CALLED

TO BEGIN YOUR DAY
with Jesus

In the morning, O Lord, You will hear my voice;
In the morning I will order my prayer to You and eagerly watch. . . .
Let all who take refuge in You be glad,
Let them ever sing for joy;
And may You shelter them,
That those who love Your name may exult in You.
For it is You who blesses the righteous man, O Lord,
You surround him with favor as with a shield.

—PSALM 5:3, 11–12

Father, thank You for this new morning and the privilege of beginning this day with You. Thank You for Your love, grace, provision, and power for those I love and for myself. I dedicate this day to You for Your service and glory. Lead me in the center of Your will. As today unfolds, give me wisdom to handle every situation I encounter as You would. Let my speech be seasoned with grace and my conduct be worthy of the name of Jesus.

I am grateful to know that regardless of what happens or where this day takes me, You will be right there with me. I am Your servant; give me understanding, that I may know You more. Establish my footsteps, and do not let any iniquity have dominion over me. Help me to live with my mind set on things above, and work through me so that Your light will shine through my life and people will be drawn to You.

May the thoughts of my mind, the words of my mouth, the meditations of my heart, the works of my hands, the paths of my feet, and the fruit of my life be not only pleasing in Your sight but in complete, joyful adherence to Your will, Father. You, Lord, are the strength of my heart and my portion forever.

In Jesus's name I pray. Amen.

TO END YOUR DAY
with Jesus

Meditate in your heart upon your bed, and be still.　　*Selah.*
Offer the sacrifices of righteousness,
And trust in the LORD*. . . .*

Lift up the light of Your countenance upon us, O LORD*!*
You have put gladness in my heart,
More than when their grain and new wine abound.
In peace I will both lie down and sleep,
For You alone, O LORD*, make me to dwell in safety.*

　　　　　　　　　—PSALM 4:4–8

Father, as today comes to an end, I thank You for all the ways You have provided for and protected my loved ones and me. Thank You for giving me wisdom and grace for everything I faced. Remind me of all You have taught me, set me back on the path of Your will wherever I have strayed, and work in my spirit so I can know and love You more.

Father, in Psalm 127:2 You promise that You grant sleep to Your beloved. Please restore my body and mind so that I can wake up tomorrow refreshed and renewed with a heart ready to serve You. I thank You that I can rest in peace because You never slumber. I am humbled that the One who lit every star in the sky watches over, cares for, and loves me unconditionally. How wonderful it is to know You and find true rest in Your everlasting arms. I am so grateful that no matter what happens tomorrow, You remain consistent and unchanging and my future is safely in Your hands.

In Jesus's name I pray. Amen.

TO ACCOMPLISH
More than You're Capable Of

He has said to me, "My grace is sufficient for you, for power is perfected in weakness." Most gladly, therefore, I will rather boast about my weaknesses, so that the power of Christ may dwell in me.

—2 CORINTHIANS 12:9

Father, how grateful I am that I can approach You with any burden or need. Lord, You know how much I have to get done and how far this undertaking is beyond my own natural abilities to accomplish. I confess this is all too much and that I am inadequate for the tasks before me. Yet, Lord, nothing is too difficult for You. So I humbly seek Your help for every bit of it. Thank You that it is no problem for You. Thank You that this is an opportunity to see Your power at work and to help me rely on You more.

I praise You, Father, for all the times in Scripture when You allowed Your people to face challenges that were greater than they could overcome on their own. I think of how Gideon was challenged with the immense armies of the Midianites and the Amalekites with only three hundred men. Yet You gave him and the people of Israel the overwhelming victory. I consider the awesome work You did through Nehemiah. Although Jerusalem had helplessly lain in ruin for more than 140 years, You gave "the people . . . a mind to work"

(Nehemiah 4:6), and the city's walls were rebuilt in just fifty-two days. And I call to mind how You allowed the disciples to feed five thousand men and their families with only five loaves and two fish.

What You did in those situations is astounding, Lord! You multiplied their strength, wisdom, desire, time, ability, and supplies. You took their meager resources and worked through them for Your glory. So, Father, I ask You to do the same with me. Multiply my time, talents, supplies, and wisdom. Give me swiftness, skillfulness, insight, and creativity. Work through me and do what only You can do.

Father, in this I know my own hand can't deliver me—all honor, glory, power, and praise are Yours. Thank You so much for helping me and that I can always have confidence in You.

In Jesus's name I pray. Amen.

TO BE
a Witness

All authority has been given to Me in heaven and on earth. Go therefore and make disciples of all the nations, baptizing them in the name of the Father and the Son and the Holy Spirit, teaching them to observe all that I commanded you; and lo, I am with you always, even to the end of the age.

—MATTHEW 28:18–20

Father, I know it is Your desire for me to be Your witness in this world—to tell others about Your good news of salvation and help them know Jesus as their Lord and Savior. This is a conviction I have received through Your Word, so I know it is Your will. I ask You to break my heart for the lost and to help me be a living testimony for You.

In Jesus's name, grant me the wisdom and courage to boldly tell others about You. Many people are on track to be separated from You forever in hell. Please prepare their hearts to accept Your salvation. Awaken unbelievers to their desire for Your presence and help them understand it is available only through Your death and resurrection, Lord Jesus. Please provide divine appointments so I can preach Your gospel and lead others to You. By Your Holy Spirit, guide me to those who long to know You, and give me the words they need to hear.

Lord Jesus, I want to be the kind of person You talk about in Matthew 5:16: "Let your light shine before men in such a way that they may see your good works, and glorify your Father who is in heaven." I want my life to bring You glory, honor, and praise. Help me to reflect

You. Cleanse me of any sinful behaviors and attitudes, and teach me to walk in Your ways. May the fruit of Your Holy Spirit flow through me—love, joy, peace, patience, kindness, goodness, faithfulness, gentleness, and self-control—to bless others.

Jesus, You said, "The harvest is plentiful, but the laborers are few" (Luke 10:2). Send me out, Lord. Work through me, and by Your mighty, supernatural, resurrection power, convict others of their sins so that they may wholeheartedly turn from their ways to Yours. Thank You for hearing my prayer, Lord Jesus. Thank You for drawing the lost to salvation. And thank You for inviting me to participate in Your great, eternal work. I look forward to taking part in Your great harvest and eagerly anticipate all You will do.

In Jesus's name I pray. Amen.

TO BE
More Loving

Love is patient, love is kind and is not jealous; love does not brag and is not arrogant, does not act unbecomingly; it does not seek its own, is not provoked, does not take into account a wrong suffered, does not rejoice in unrighteousness, but rejoices with the truth; bears all things, believes all things, hopes all things, endures all things.

Love never fails.

—1 CORINTHIANS 13:4–8

Lord Jesus, I have read where You've said, "By this all men will know that you are My disciples, if you have love for one another" (John 13:35). Yet I've realized, Lord, that many times, I have not responded to others in love. Rather, I've found myself disliking or having conflicts with people, judging them and demanding my rights rather than showing them grace. Please forgive me, Father. I know I am not reflecting Your character—and it is hurting my witness for You.

Therefore, Jesus, I ask You to please make me more caring. Teach me how to lay down my life for others, showing them unconditional love as You do. I realize this is not something I can work up on my own but is the fruit of Your Holy Spirit. So, Lord, I submit myself to You to make me kinder and more patient. Purge any need to impress others, jealousy, arrogance, pride, or unbecoming behavior in me. Father, whatever is selfish in me or easily provoked—please heal it. Show me how to be more tenderhearted, forgiving, and compassionate.

Lord, I confess that I have rejoiced when people I don't like fail—please forgive me. Help me to rejoice with the truth instead. I will root for everyone to mature in their faith, trust You more, and experience Your freedom and victory.

Father, empower me to bear all things, remembering that everyone I meet is someone You love and has hidden inadequacies, fears, and battles that deserve my compassion. Help me always to believe the best about people, hope and pray for Your breakthroughs in their lives, and have a love for them that endures even when wronged. Lord Jesus, You never fail, so help me not to falter in glorifying You by caring for others.

Thank You, Jesus, for making me a channel of Your love to those I meet. And thank You for never leaving or forsaking me. I owe so much to Your unconditional love—to the great sacrifices You've made for me and the immense blessings You've given me. Help me live my life in loving thanks to You.

In Jesus's name I pray. Amen.

TO BE
More like Jesus

Those whom He foreknew, He also predestined to become con-formed to the image of His Son, so that He would be the firstborn among many brethren; and these whom He predestined, He also called; and these whom He called, He also justified; and these whom He justified, He also glorified.

—ROMANS 8:29–30

Lord God Almighty, thank You for saving me and call-ing me Your own. I am so grateful I am to be Your child, endowed with every spiritual blessing. Out of a thankful heart, Father, I desire to walk in Your will and in a manner that pleases You. I realize this means that You will root out the attitudes and habits that no longer fit me as a believer and conform me to the likeness of Jesus. Therefore, Father, I submit to You and affirm my desire to present my body as a living and holy sacrifice as an act of worship to You.

Transform my character to be more like You, Jesus. Help me think as You do and behave in a manner that exalts You so others can believe and be saved. I turn my thoughts and my ways over to You, Lord. Teach me how to live in Your freedom, releasing me from the bondage of sin so I can walk in Your liberty. Fill me with the confidence that You demonstrated as You walked on the earth—Your unwavering com-mitment to the course, Your unshakable faith, and Your unfaltering assurance that all Your Word will be fulfilled.

Lord Jesus, I want to be conformed to Your example of obedience —being submitted to Your plan regardless of the obstacles, challenges, or sacrifices. Give me Your heart for others, Lord, which demonstrates self-sacrificing grace, compassion, and love. Make me passionate for Your holiness. Help me always to be fully focused on You—accomplishing Your plans in Your ways and timing—and not disheartened or defeated because of trials.

Show me my part in Your mission—helping others to know and experience You in an eternal, unbroken relationship and become Your fully devoted followers. And empower me, Lord Jesus, through the presence of Your Holy Spirit, that the very power of the resurrection may be demonstrated in and through my life so that others might know You, the Living God.

In every way, Lord Jesus, make me like You. In my conversation, conduct, and character, may people sense Your presence, see Your light, and glorify You.

In Jesus's name I pray. Amen.

TO CLAIM A
Promise

Blessed be the Lᴀᴀᴀ *, who has given rest to His people Israel, according to all that He promised; not one word has failed of all His good promise.*

—1 KINGS 8:56

Lord God, how wonderful Your Word and how great the promises You have made to those who love You and walk according to Your purposes. Thank You for leading me on the path of Your will through Scripture and teaching me Your ways. Truly, You are good, kind, and faithful.

Father, as I have been reading Your Word, Your promise in [Scripture reference] has been on my heart and has come to mind many times. Therefore, Lord, I ask You to show me if this is a promise I can apply to my life. And if so, how do I do so in a manner that honors You? Show me, Father. Confirm Your promise to me.

Help me always to focus on the realities and principles that uphold Your promises, Father. You reveal Yourself through them and draw me closer to You, and Your wisdom, power, and faithful character allow them to be fulfilled. In other words, Lord Jesus, the purpose of a promise is to exalt You, the great Promise Keeper. So as I personally claim Your scriptural assurances, help me not to be so wrapped up in what You will give but in who You are.

Lord Jesus, I know You are faithful to fulfill all Your great and wonderful Word. I trust, my Lord and my God, that You have a good, acceptable, and perfect plan for my life. I choose Your purposes above my own, Father. Help me to walk in Your will and exalt You in all things.

In Jesus's name I pray. Amen.

TO DO WHAT
Doesn't Make Sense

"My thoughts are not your thoughts,
Nor are your ways My ways," declares the LORD.
"For as the heavens are higher than the earth,
So are My ways higher than your ways
And My thoughts than your thoughts.
For as the rain and the snow come down from heaven,
And do not return there without watering the earth
And making it bear and sprout,
And furnishing seed to the sower and bread to the eater;
So will My word be which goes forth from My mouth;
It will not return to Me empty,
Without accomplishing what I desire,
And without succeeding in the matter for which I sent it."

—ISAIAH 55:8–11

Father, thank You for loving me and leading me in all things. Lord, as I have sought You in these last days and months through Your Word and in prayer, I sense You calling me to obey You in ways I do not fully understand and that are far beyond my natural abilities. I know You are asking me to step out in faith—trusting You even though I don't have a full picture of how You will fulfill Your plans for me. Lord Jesus, I declare that I believe You and I will obey You.

Like Abraham setting out from Ur of the Chaldees not knowing where he was going, I will do as You say and take this step with confidence in You. I will not let my heart be swayed from following You by obstacles or challenges, Father. Rather, I will do what You say and leave the consequences to You. I know this is an awesome opportunity for You to demonstrate Your faithfulness and love, build my character, and deepen our relationship. I also recognize that in Your economy, what You promise is already fulfilled. So I thank You now, Father, for bringing all Your promises to fruition.

Father, please give me Your wisdom and guide me every step of the way. I thank You for the examples of Joseph, Moses, David, and Paul, who all went forward in faith and found You to be trustworthy, good, powerful, and wise. I thank You for the truth of Your Word by which You guide me. Help me to stay strong, recalling past successes, rejecting discouraging words, recognizing the spiritual nature of the battles I face, responding to trials with a positive confession, relying on Your power, and reckoning the victory. I know I can face any circumstance with confidence and hope because triumph comes from Your hand.

So I rejoice in You, Lord, and all You will do. How grateful I am that we go together in this adventure and that no matter what happens, You are with me. To You be the glory in this situation and in every aspect of my life.

In Jesus's name I pray. Amen.

TO FIND A
Church Home

Let us consider how to stimulate one another to love and good deeds, not forsaking our own assembling together, as is the habit of some, but encouraging one another; and all the more as you see the day drawing near.

—HEBREWS 10:24–25

Father, thank You for adopting me into Your family and giving me Christian brothers and sisters with whom to walk through life. How grateful I am that You have not called me to "go it alone" but have planned in advance for me to have a support system as I mature in my faith. Thank You, Father, that You already know where You desire me to join and serve. Lead me to a church home where I can worship You in spirit and truth.

Father, as I visit churches, I rely on Your guidance. Please help me discern whether a church is healthy, ministry-minded, and growing. Make me sensitive to the doctrines of the church—whether they believe Jesus is the only way of salvation; the Bible is Your Word; the virgin birth, bodily resurrection, and second coming of Jesus are true; that there's a time for each person to stand before You and give an account; and that heaven and hell are real. Guide me to a church where my family and I can grow in our faith, be strengthened in our relationship with You, learn and understand more about Scripture, serve in the gifts You have given us, and experience You together. I also pray for a church that is both evangelistic and missions-minded—making a difference both in the local community and around the world for Your kingdom with the good news of salvation.

Thank You, Father, for leading me to a church that will teach me about and exalt Jesus, be my support group in difficult times, and teach me how to serve You with my whole life. And make me a good church member, Father—one that promotes unity, overflows with the fruit of the Spirit, and follows You wholeheartedly. Thank You, Lord, for Your Body. I look forward to all You will do through us together.

In Jesus's name I pray. Amen.

TO INTERCEDE FOR
Your Children

Behold, children are a gift of the LORD,
The fruit of the womb is a reward.
Like arrows in the hand of a warrior,
So are the children of one's youth.

—PSALM 127:3-4

Father, thank You for being such a beautiful example of the kind of parent I ought to be. You love us, forgive us, instruct us, listen to us, provide for us, and set boundaries for our protection. And You call each of us into a personal relationship with You. Heavenly Father, You are so kind and patient. Thank You for loving my children even more than I do and having wonderful plans for their lives.

The first thing I pray for my children is that they would know You as Savior—with a faith that's their own. Thank You for giving me the opportunity to lead them and build biblical foundations into their lives. Please give me the desire, energy, and wisdom to invest in them so that they can experience the lifelong blessing of walking in obedience to You. Each child is unique in personality and giftedness; therefore, please give me the insight and discernment to minister to each one individually—even as You do, Father. At each stage of their lives, endow me with an appreciation for how You have formed them, and show me how best to bring out all the good gifts You have placed in them for Your glory. And when they have heartache and struggle, do not allow me to increase their burdens. Rather, help me to be an instrument of Your peace, pointing them to You.

Enable me to provide a godly home so my children will learn to honor and glorify You throughout their lives. Help me teach my children to seek You as Lord, instilling in them a love for Your Word and an understanding of how beautiful, personal, and powerful prayer can be. Jesus, I pray that my children will follow Your example, be conformed to Your character, and seek opportunities to represent You to others. May they mature in their walk, worship, and witness. Teach them to be wise, humble, and holy, Lord Jesus—full of the fruit of Your Spirit. And provide them with godly friends and influences who will help them serve You well.

Please spiritually awaken our family, make each of us wholly devoted to You, and bind us even closer together. And, Father, in all the ways my family doesn't experience You fully, I pray that You will show me where I am not being the parent I need to be. Guide me by Your Holy Spirit to understand the behaviors and attitudes that undermine my children's well-being. Help me always to view my children as blessings and view myself as their steward—committing to do whatever is necessary to keep my kids on Your team.

I pray that my children will grow in Your grace, mature in their faith, exalt You with their gifts, and testify boldly about You to others. Let their light so shine before others, that they may see their good works and glorify You, our Father in heaven. I know this is Your will according to Your Word. Thank You for all You will do through them, Lord, and for Your amazing faithfulness.

In Jesus's name I pray. Amen.

TO INTERCEDE
for the Lost

Seeing the people, He felt compassion for them, because they were distressed and dispirited like sheep without a shepherd. Then He said to His disciples, "The harvest is plentiful, but the workers are few. Therefore beseech the Lord of the harvest to send out workers into His harvest."

—MATTHEW 9:36–38

Lord Jesus, how grateful I am that You hear my prayers. I praise You for being so near to those who seek You. Thank You for cleansing me of my sin through Your death and resurrection. How I long for more people to take hold of Your grace. Therefore, Father, I pray for the lost and ask You to prepare their hearts to accept Your salvation. Stir in unbelievers a desire for Your presence, and help them understand it is available only through the death and resurrection of the Lord Jesus.

Father, every day people experience events that cause them to ask questions. They become frightened, face needs, and feel confusion and hurt. Their hearts cry out for answers, Lord, but they seek solutions to their pain in places that offer only empty, temporary relief. Lord Jesus, please show the lost that the way, the truth, and the life can be found only in You. Please place me and other Christians in their path.

You have called believers to be Your ambassadors here on earth— You call us by Your own name. Yet we have not always represented You well. Father, help us humble ourselves, stir us to pray, make us hungry for Your presence, and show us the wickedness of our ways so that we may turn from them. Shine Your light through our lives. But also help us to be bold in our witness to this lost and dying world.

By Your Holy Spirit, give us divine appointments wherever we go, Father, that we may preach Your gospel and that many may be saved. Indeed, Lord, You always give what is good, and Your Word never returns void—it always accomplishes Your desires. Therefore, fill our mouths with Your message. Guide our footsteps to those who long to know You, and give us the words to reach their hearts with Your truth.

Thank You for salvation, for hearing my prayer, and for softening the hearts of the lost. Thank You for bringing spiritual awakening to many who need You. I thank You for every knee that bows and every tongue that confesses that Jesus is Lord, to the glory of God the Father. For You, my Savior, are worthy of all the honor, power, and praise, now and forevermore.

In Jesus's name I pray. Amen.

TO LOVE
Jesus More

*You shall love the Lord your God with all your heart, and with
all your soul, and with all your mind, and with all your strength.*
—MARK 12:30

Lord, I want to love You more. How grateful I am to know that
this is a prayer You desire to answer. I realize that the issues I have in
trusting and obeying You are because I don't know and care for You
as deeply as I should. Therefore, Father, I set my heart to seek Your
face and yearn to have a more profound, intimate understanding of
Your ways, Your will, and who You are. Reveal Yourself, Lord Jesus.
As I open Your Word and kneel before You in prayer, show me Your
wonderful face. I want to truly know You.

Thank You for loving me and leading me to love You more. I confess I have not always acted in a caring manner toward You. I have
needed You, leaned on You, called on You in times of crisis—but not
always out of love. And yet You have always answered me with compassion and mercy. Forgive me, Father. Thank You for not treating me the
way I often treat You, but always leading me with kindness, wisdom,
and grace.

So today I do not seek You out of fear or selfishness, for any need or
problem. I just want You. I declare as Paul did, "I count all things to be
loss in view of the surpassing value of knowing Christ Jesus my Lord"
(Philippians 3:8). I long to spend time with You and find joy in Your
presence. I yearn to please and worship You, my Redeemer and King.

I love You, Lord Jesus. Thank You for being my Savior and giving me the privilege of a relationship with You. Whatever You desire from me, the answer is yes. Thank You for hearing my prayer.

In Jesus's name I pray. Amen.

TO OBEY GOD
When It's Costly

Offer to God a sacrifice of thanksgiving
And pay your vows to the Most High;
Call upon Me in the day of trouble;
I shall rescue you, and you will honor Me.
—PSALM 50:14–15

Lord God, thank You for saving me, calling me Your own, and giving me purpose. Thank You for speaking through Your Word and guiding me in the decisions I must make. Lord, You know this step is difficult because of how much it will cost me and those I love. I realize You are calling me to step out in faith—trusting not only that You can truly supply all my needs but also that there is a reward when I seek and obey You.

I affirm that my desire is to submit to You and walk in Your will. But I also confess my fears, Father, and the temptation to dwell on the cost rather than to focus on You and have faith. Please help me. I ask You to confirm that this is indeed the path I should take. Give me promises I can cling to so I will not falter or lose heart when challenges arise or answers delay. Bestow me with the grace and wisdom to do all You ask, and empower me to do Your will.

Lord, my answer to You is yes. Regardless of the cost, I will obey, acknowledging that You are the Lord God Almighty—my Savior, Redeemer, and King. You have created me and purchased my life and are worthy of my devotion. You are my hope, my life, my all. I step out

183

in faith, leaning on Your everlasting arms. Thank You for never failing or forsaking me; rather, You always lead me to Your very best. I will trust in You. May my life bring You honor, glory, and praise.

In Jesus's name I pray. Amen.

TO OBEY GOD
When Others Don't Understand

Am I now seeking the favor of men, or of God? Or am I striving to please men? If I were still trying to please men, I would not be a bond-servant of Christ.

—GALATIANS 1:10

Lord Jesus, I thank You for Your presence in my life and how You have been guiding me in Your will. Despite the challenges, difficulties, and disappointments, I know You are at work and that the path You have for me is good. Yet I confess that at times I feel alone because my loved ones do not understand the course You have laid out for me or the manner in which You have gifted me.

Lord Jesus, the pressure from others can be great and disheartening. But I trust in Your wisdom. Thank You for sympathizing with me, understanding my struggles, and being my Great High Priest. You know my most profound questions, lofty dreams, and deepest hurts. You intercede for me at the throne of grace and give me mercy and help in my time of need. What gives me the most comfort is that You have experienced everything I have—rejection, ridicule, and even hardships within Your earthly family—and yet overcame it all without sinning. Thank You for having compassion on me and teaching me how to walk in a manner that honors You.

Jesus, thank You for always being with me, even when all others abandon me. Thank You for protecting me, providing for me, and empowering me to carry out Your will. I praise You because You have the best plan—one unmatched by any other on earth—and You enable me to live life at its best. I will do as You ask. To You be all the praise.

In Jesus's name I pray. Amen.

TO EXHIBIT THE
Fruit of the Spirit

The fruit of the Spirit is love, joy, peace, patience, kindness, goodness, faithfulness, gentleness, self-control.
—GALATIANS 5:22–23

Father, how grateful I am that You desire to live Your life through me. Thank You for conforming me to the image of Jesus and helping me be more like You in every way. You change my desires, needs, habits, innermost goals, and even the patterns by which I operate as I walk with You. Thank You that even though it takes time and intentional effort to change the thinking and behaviors that are ingrained within me, You never give up.

Lord, when I read about the fruit of Your Spirit and Your commands about how to relate to others, I am aware of how often I fall short. I want to be as loving, joyful, peaceful, patient, kind, good, faithful, gentle, and self-controlled as You are. I realize these aren't response patterns I can change on my own but that require Your supernatural intervention because they are counter to who I am in my flesh. Only You can transform me inside out so that these attributes can flow through me.

Therefore, Jesus, I set my heart to cooperate with You. You said, "I am the vine, you are the branches; he who abides in Me and I in him, he bears much fruit, for apart from Me you can do nothing" (John 15:5). I affirm that, Lord Jesus. Your life pouring into me is what enables me to live the Christian life and bear the hallmarks of character that are the fruit of Your Spirit. So teach me to abide in You so that Your fruit can always be produced through me to Your glory. Show me if there is any ungodliness in me, that I may repent and walk in Your ways.

Thank You, Lord Jesus, for giving me Your Holy Spirit to help me. Thank You not only for conferring Your holiness to me through the cross but also for transforming me into a vessel of that holy life and enabling me to live it. I submit myself to You. To You be all honor, glory, power, and praise forever.

In Jesus's name I pray. Amen.

TO INTERCEDE FOR
Your Country

*If My people who are called by My name will humble themselves,
and pray and seek My face, and turn from their wicked ways,
then I will hear from heaven, and will forgive their sin and heal
their land.*

—2 CHRONICLES 7:14 NKJV

Father, thank You for the country You have chosen to be my home. In Your grace, You decided where I would be born, how I would come to know You as my Savior, and where I would serve You. Thank You, Lord God. Today I ask You to open my eyes to see this nation as You see it. Give my fellow citizens and me sorrow for those things that sadden Your heart and the resolve to repent of our sinful ways, that we might draw closer to You and experience more of Your presence, provision, and protection. Show us how to rely solely on the eternal hope You give us, rather than the empty optimism of this world.

Help us, Lord, to get on track and to embrace the purposes You planned for us as a nation. Send a spiritual awakening to the citizens and bring a revival of Your church. Forgive us, Lord, for allowing rampant immorality to engulf us as a nation, and show us how to put an end to the unrighteousness in our land—starting with our own hearts and minds. Purify us and refine us as Your people, that we might reflect Your glory and lead others to You. Give believers the courage to speak up and stand for what is right in Your sight. Teach us Your words, and may our message pierce the hearts of our fellow citizens with Your truth. Help us to be salt and light so many will know You as Savior.

Father, I pray that You would draw the leaders of this nation to Yourself in renewed humility and faith. May those who do not know You accept Jesus as their Lord and Savior. Create a desire for greater accountability—both in our own lives and in those of our leaders. Speak to our lawmakers as only You can. Convict them of their responsibility—first to You and second to the people You have allowed them to lead. And free them from the bondage to destructive ideologies that would lead us away from You. Show us, Lord, who deserves our vote. Help us elect the men and women You desire to work through in the coming years.

Protect us from enemies both foreign and domestic. Likewise, heavenly Father, please show us the way out of debt. Save us from the burden of overtaxation, and put our nation back to work. Give us a renewed understanding about our responsibilities toward one another, and restore our desire to help those in need.

Lord God, bring us to our knees as a nation. Teach us to pray. Show us Your power, love, and wisdom as we bow before You. Father, we have faith that You can move mightily and that You will do awesome things as we humble ourselves before You. We have confidence that You will show us what to do. Please give us the strength and knowledge to carry out Your marvelous plans. Draw us close to You, and help us intercede for our country and leaders. Guide us in Your love so that we can generously and faithfully direct others to You and be a light to the world. We look to You and count on Your grace today and every day. To You be all the honor, glory, power, and praise in this nation and in every country on earth.

In Jesus's name I pray. Amen.

TO SUPPORT
Israel

Pray for the peace of Jerusalem:
"May they prosper who love you.
May peace be within your walls,
And prosperity within your palaces."
—PSALM 122:6–7

God of Abraham, Isaac, and Jacob, You keep Your covenants to a thousand generations and have never failed to keep Your Word to Your people. Thank You for being so faithful to Israel and for keeping Your promise to reestablish her in the land You've given her as an inheritance. Lord, You are Israel's Defender and King and have worked miracles on her behalf. Thank You for this nation that You have chosen as a platform for Your glorious work.

I pray for Israel as a nation. May her leaders be like King David—men and women after Your own heart who will do Your will regardless of the cost. Father, convict them against infighting and corruption, and help them work together for the welfare of the country. Thank You for the prosperity and wisdom You have given the Jewish people. Israel stands in the world as a technological and military wonder—and that is due to the favor You've given her. I pray that the nations of the world would take Your covenants with Israel seriously, understanding that You bless those who support her and curse those who oppose her. Truly, Jerusalem has become a cup of trembling for all the nations. Defend her against attack, Lord—securing her borders, protecting her from foreign and domestic enemies, giving her peace, and endowing her with favor when other nations debate her future. I praise You that no country or confederacy can do anything against her apart from Your permission.

How blessed and favored is Israel that You—the Lord and Savior of all humanity, Jesus Christ—have come from her. Thank You, Lord Jesus, that all the people of the earth have been offered the gift of salvation through Your death on the cross and resurrection. May the people of Israel acknowledge their guilt, seek Your face, and accept Jesus as the Messiah they have been waiting for. Turn the hearts of all Jews throughout the world back to Yourself, Lord God, and may a great spiritual awakening break out among Your chosen people. Likewise, I pray that even Israel's enemies would know You as Lord and Savior and through You have everlasting peace.

May Christians from around the world acknowledge Your continuing special relationship with Israel, stand with and bless the Jewish people, pray for the peace of Jerusalem, fight anti-Semitism in all its forms, and renounce theologies that deny the unconditional promises You've made to the descendants of Abraham. Thank You, Lord Jesus, for hearing my prayers and for keeping all Your promises to the Jewish people.

In Jesus's name I pray. Amen.

TO INTERCEDE FOR
Worldwide Revival and Spiritual Awakening

Revive us, and we will call upon Your name.
O LORD God of hosts, restore us;
Cause Your face to shine upon us, and we will be saved.
—PSALM 80:18–19

Lord God Almighty, You are worthy of all worship and praise. Yet I know, Father, that many still do not know You as Savior, and in many areas Your church is struggling. Therefore, Father, I come before You to ask for Your intervention—help us exalt You. Revive Your church throughout the world, and send a spiritual awakening among all who do not yet know Jesus as Savior.

Forgive us, Lord God, for the way Your people have drifted from You. Bring Your church to the place where we have the courage to admit that we do not have all the answers, we have made mistakes, and we have become too much like the world. Guide us into Your wisdom, and teach us to do Your will. We long to trust You completely in all things and to follow You in obedience so others can know You and be saved.

Almighty God, please give Your people a hunger for Your presence and a thirst for Your righteousness and a boldness for proclaiming Your Word. Drive us to Scripture so we might know You anew. Help us to hear Your voice, and direct us by Your Holy Spirit so we can walk in the center of Your will and be perfectly aligned to Your purposes. Please speak unity and peace to us, Your people, so that we may carry the good news of Jesus Christ to those who are lost and perishing. Let us not turn back to folly, Father, destroying our testimonies to the people around us. Rather, teach us to carry Your message with loving-kindness, truth, righteousness, and gentleness to the uttermost parts of the earth.

We ask You to prepare the hearts of the lost to accept Your salvation. Awaken unbelievers to their desire for Your presence, and help them understand it is available only through the death and resurrection of our Lord Jesus Christ. Give us divine appointments wherever we go, Father, that we may preach Your gospel and that many will be saved. Send believers to the unreached—yes, even to areas antagonistic to You—so that people from every nation, tribe, and tongue will worship You.

Indeed, Lord, You always give what is good, and Your Word never returns void—it always yields its produce. By Your Holy Spirit, guide our footsteps to those who long to know You, and give us the words they need to hear. Our hearts long to see every nation throughout the earth praise Your holy and wonderful name. The loving-kindness You have shown us is beyond measure, and we desire for people everywhere to know Your eternal provision of salvation through Jesus Christ.

So, Lord, please make Your people a light to the nations and an example of the Savior's love and grace. May the lost come to understand the spiritual freedom from sin that You have so graciously provided for us. We give praise for all You are doing and will do. Thank You for reviving the church throughout the world and for bringing spiritual awakening to unbelievers. To You be all honor, glory, and worship now and forevermore.

In Jesus's name I pray. Amen.

TO LOVE YOUR
Enemies

Love your enemies, do good to those who hate you, bless those who curse you, pray for those who mistreat you. Whoever hits you on the cheek, offer him the other also; and whoever takes away your coat, do not withhold your shirt from him either. Give to everyone who asks of you, and whoever takes away what is yours, do not demand it back. Treat others the same way you want them to treat you.... Love your enemies, and do good, and lend, expecting nothing in return; and your reward will be great, and you will be sons of the Most High; for He Himself is kind to ungrateful and evil men.

—LUKE 6:27–31, 35

Father, thank You for safeguarding me and for giving me refuge under Your wings of protection. Truly, Your faithfulness has been a shield and bulwark for me. I know that no one can touch my life apart from Your will. Therefore, I will not be afraid. But, Father, You call me to pray for my enemies and show them love. So I will obey You in this, my Lord and my God.

Lord, first I ask You to shield my heart with Your forgiveness. Do not allow me to be resentful or angry, because that would give the Enemy a foothold. I repent of any bitterness that has already taken hold within me. Rather, Father, I count on the fact that You are my Shield and Defender and have promised, "No weapon that is formed against you will prosper; and every tongue that accuses you in judgment you will condemn. This is the heritage of the servants of the LORD, and their vindication is from Me" (Isaiah 54:17). Therefore, Father, help me always to be a good witness.

That said, Lord, I turn my prayer to the condition of the ones who have attacked me. You love them, even if they have not yet accepted You as Lord and Savior. You created them, even if they aren't serving You. So break my heart for them, Jesus—for the wounds within them that cause them to strike out as they have toward me. Help me always remember that so much of what goes on within the human heart is a spiritual battle, and often people act as they do for reasons that are unknown even to themselves.

Therefore, Lord Jesus, please draw them to You, show them Your truth, and if they do not yet know You as Savior, reveal Your salvation to them in a powerful way. Convict them of their sin so they can repent and walk in Your will. Heal their wounds, and show Yourself powerful on their behalf. Remove the bitterness and fill them with Your love. Give them hope and purpose. They need You, Lord. They need to know You and have Your powerful work in their lives. So forgive them, for they know not what they do. And if You want to work through me as an instrument of Your peace, show me how I can bless them and do good on their behalf.

God Most High, turn my enemies into friends so we can praise You together. Thank You for hearing my prayers and for being my unfailing tower of strength and safety. To You be all the glory now and forever.

In Jesus's name I pray. Amen.

TO PUT ON
Spiritual Armor

Be strong in the Lord and in the strength of His might. Put on the full armor of God, so that you will be able to stand firm against the schemes of the devil. For our struggle is not against flesh and blood, but against the rulers, against the powers, against the world forces of this darkness, against the spiritual forces of wickedness in the heavenly places.

—EPHESIANS 6:10–12

Father, thank You for offering me Your strength and for clothing me in Your mighty power. Thank You for giving me Your unbreakable, impenetrable armor so that I am able to serve You and stand firm against all strategies of the devil. Help me always to remember that I am not fighting against flesh-and-blood enemies but against evil rulers and authorities of the unseen world, against mighty powers of darkness, and against evil spirits in the heavenly places.

Father, You command me to take up Your armor, so affix it to me, Lord, that I may be able to resist the Enemy in the time of evil and can steadfastly endure all that happens. Help me stand my ground by putting on the belt of truth, which guards against the Enemy's lies, and Your righteousness, which protects me from the Enemy's traps. For shoes, I ask that You would adorn me with the peace that comes from the good news so that I will be fully prepared to represent You well to everyone I meet. May the mission of the gospel carry me wherever I go.

In addition, help me hold up the shield of faith to stop all the fiery arrows of the devil. His desire is to strike me to the heart to discourage me, but I will trust in You. Father, guard my mind with the salvation You've given me as my helmet, and help me take up the sword of the Spirit, which is Your Word. Lord, bring verses to my mind to fight off the Enemy's attacks.

Help me to pray in the Spirit at all times and on every occasion, and make me sensitive to the Enemy's tactics and onslaughts. Show me how to stay alert and be persistent in my prayers for all believers everywhere, especially my brothers and sisters in the persecuted church. And, Father, give me the right words so I can courageously and lovingly explain Your wonderful plan to everyone I meet. Whatever difficulties may arise or the challenges, adversities, or sorrows that assail, help my loved ones and me to keep on speaking boldly for You, as we should.

In Jesus's name I pray. Amen.

TO
Repent

Seek the LORD while you can find him.
   Call on him now while he is near.
Let the wicked change their ways
   and banish the very thought of doing wrong.
Let them turn to the LORD that he may have mercy on them.
   Yes, turn to our God, for he will forgive generously.
—ISAIAH 55:6–7 NLT

Father, I know You are drawing me into Your presence and calling me to repent. Something is between You and me—something that is undermining both our relationship and my life. Be gracious, O God, by examining my heart and revealing my sins. According to Your loving-kindness and the greatness of Your compassion, show me where I have strayed from Your will so I may confess my transgressions to You and know the freedom of Your forgiveness. Make me clean before You so I can continue to walk with You, Father.

Father, I wait before You and listen. As You reveal my iniquity, I confess it. I have [confess your transgressions to God]. Thank You for showing me, by the inner conviction of Your Holy Spirit, where I have sinned against You. I want to obey You and walk in a manner worthy of You. Therefore, Father, I ask You to show me how to break free from the behavioral and thought patterns that make me fall to temptation. Reveal the lies that cause me to fall, replace them with Your truth, and show me how to walk in Your will. As You address the ungodly ways in me, I will obey You, even when I don't understand completely.

Thank You for alerting me to my sin, forgiving me, cleansing my heart, and conforming me to the likeness of the Lord Jesus. Thank You for getting me back on Your path, Father. May I honor You in all my ways.

In Jesus's name I pray. Amen.

TO SERVICE—
Using Your Gifts for God's Glory

As each one has received a special gift, employ it in serving one another as good stewards of the manifold grace of God. Whoever speaks, is to do so as one who is speaking the utterances of God; whoever serves is to do so as one who is serving by the strength which God supplies; so that in all things God may be glorified through Jesus Christ, to whom belongs the glory and dominion forever and ever. Amen.

—1 PETER 4:10–11

Father, how grateful I am that You have saved me, sanctified me, and empowered me to serve You. I know from Your Word that You have given me spiritual gifts, talents, and blessings that are to be used in Your service for the edification of others. Lord God, I submit myself to You and place all of who I am on the altar for Your use. May my service to You become a spiritual act of worship—exalting You for who You are.

Father, I don't know all the ways You desire to work through me. Therefore, Lord, I ask that You reveal how I can best serve You and Your people. Give me discernment to know which opportunities are truly from You. Help me to fit in to the body of Christ in unity, and endow me with wisdom about how to minister in Your name.

Father, may my love for You and for others overflow more and more. Help me to keep on growing in knowledge and understanding, remaining focused on what really matters, so that I can live a pure and blameless life before You until the day of Christ's return. Deliver me from pride and any sinful way in me. And please fill me with the fruit of the salvation You have given me—the righteous character produced by Jesus Christ—for this will bring much glory and praise to You, our Lord and our God.

Lord, I realize that Your power is perfected in weakness. You choose to shine through my limitations to show that the surpassing power is from You and not from me. Therefore, there will be trials, distresses, and disappointments. In those times, Father, I pray that I can always keep my eyes on You and say as Paul does, "Most gladly, therefore, I will rather boast about my weaknesses, so that the power of Christ may dwell in me. Therefore I am well content with weaknesses, with insults, with distresses, with persecutions, with difficulties, for Christ's sake; for when I am weak, then I am strong" (2 Corinthians 12:9-10).

Thank You for Your indwelling Holy Spirit, who enables me to do whatever You ask. Help me understand and rely upon the incredible greatness of Your power that You have given so freely to those who believe in You. This is the same mighty power that raised You, Jesus, from the dead and seated You in the place of honor at God's right hand in the heavenly realms. You have given me resurrection power to serve You. Thank You, Lord!

Jesus, I affirm that You are far above any ruler, authority, power, or leader—not only in this world but also in the world to come. All things are under Your authority, Lord Jesus, and You are head over all things. It is good and right that I give myself to You utterly and completely. So I say, I am Your servant, my Lord and my God. Direct me for Your glory. May my life always bring You honor and praise.

In Jesus's name I pray. Amen.

TO TAKE ON A
Great Opportunity

I will bow down toward Your holy temple
And give thanks to Your name for Your lovingkindness and
*   Your truth;*
For You have magnified Your word according to all Your name.
On the day I called, You answered me;
You made me bold with strength in my soul. . . .
The LORD will accomplish what concerns me;
Your lovingkindness, O LORD, is everlasting.
                    —PSALM 138:2–3, 8

Father, thank You for being my wonderful Provider. No one could ever guess what You desire to do, because Your plans are so above and beyond all I could ask or imagine. How grateful I am for the opportunity You have set before me. I know it is from You, Lord, and I acknowledge that I must have faith in You if I desire to take hold of it. Let me not take it for granted, but help me to see all You desire to accomplish through it.

Father, I put this prospect and myself on the altar before You. May this not become an idol in my life or a situation that tempts me to pride and self-reliance. No, Lord, this is from You and for Your glory. Therefore, please show me the way I should go, and direct me with Your eye upon me so I can walk in a manner worthy of You.

Likewise, Father, I know the temptation is to see either only the positive or only the negative in situations, rather than seeing them for what they really are. Therefore, now at the threshold of this opportunity, as excitement fills my soul, help me to be sober and shrewd. Give me wisdom about how to proceed and what to reveal to others. When the road becomes difficult, Father—as it always does—empower me to endure as challenges arise and when the way ahead grows dark and confusing. Don't allow me to become negative, resentful, or full of complaining. Rather, may the trying times become opportunities to trust You and draw nearer to You.

Father, I pray that in all things, my conversation, conduct, and character will exalt You. Thank You for working through me and this opportunity for Your glory. I confess, there is some fear as I embark on this journey with You. But with courage and conviction, I go forth to serve You in this prospect, believing You enable me for it. I am Your servant. Therefore, to You, Lord God—who are able to do far more abundantly beyond all that I could ever ask or think—to You be the glory in every situation, circumstance, and opportunity forever and ever.

In Jesus's name I pray. Amen.

TO TAME YOUR
Tongue

Who is the man who desires life
And loves length of days that he may see good?
Keep your tongue from evil
And your lips from speaking deceit.
Depart from evil and do good;
Seek peace and pursue it.

—PSALM 34:12–14

Lord, You are clear throughout Scripture about the impact of our words. You even say, "Death and life are in the power of the tongue" (Proverbs 18:21). I realize, Father, that I have a great responsibility to consider what I communicate to others. This is why the apostle Paul admonishes, "Let no unwholesome word proceed from your mouth, but only such a word as is good for edification according to the need of the moment, so that it will give grace to those who hear" (Ephesians 4:29). To think of how I could be speaking either life or death to others is weighty indeed.

I ask Your forgiveness for how I have hurt people with my words. Today people say whatever they feel without restraint. But, Lord, I acknowledge that that does not reflect Your wisdom and is the path to sure ruin. Therefore, please guard my mouth so that what proceeds from it exalts You and edifies others. Help me not to speak in haste, out of anger, or because of pride. Instead, teach me to weigh my words, be a peacemaker, and always communicate the truth in love and humility. I know this change begins in my heart as You conform me to Your image. As my heart is transformed, so is the fruit of my mouth.

Therefore, Lord Jesus, sanctify me—make me into a person who speaks healing and life to others. Don't let my aim be about drawing people to myself, making my opinions known, or proving how smart I am. No, Lord, the important thing is to lead others to You. Therefore, may my speech always be seasoned with grace so that I will know how to respond to each person I meet in a manner that exalts You and encourages them. And help me to testify about You so others may find freedom in Your name. Thank You for hearing my prayer, transforming my heart, taming my tongue, and making my whole life a testimony of Your grace.

In Jesus's name I pray. Amen.

TO
Wait

I would have despaired unless I had believed that I would see
   the goodness of the LORD
In the land of the living.
Wait for the LORD;
Be strong and let your heart take courage;
Yes, wait for the LORD.

                          —PSALM 27:13–14

Father, thank You for Your precious promises and Your good plans for my life. I know You lead me in righteousness and wisdom—that You have my best interests at heart in everything that happens. Your will is good, acceptable, and perfect, and I can trust in You. Lord, I am so grateful that even when You call me to wait, I can know for certain that it is not in vain but meant for Your good and loving purposes. Thank You for being intimately involved in every detail of my life and for guiding me in Your perfect timing.

Lord Jesus, I confess that in these last days, when difficult circumstances have arisen, the pain of being denied my dreams and desires has pierced my heart. The obstacles and pressures can become overwhelming. At times, I feel trapped without recourse—imprisoned, chained, and without hope. But I know You allow only the trials that can strengthen my faith, build my character, and deepen my relationship with You.

So, Father, I thank You that with You there is always hope! I will

207

keep believing in You. I trust that You can and will help me in the situations that continually press on my heart. Lord, please reveal how You are acting on my behalf and what You desire to teach me through this time of waiting. Surround me and protect me with Your loving, powerful presence, peace, and assurance. Teach me to sit expectantly before Your glorious throne of grace, from which You show me how to walk in Your ways. And in all things, help me to honor You, seek Your face, obey Your commands, reflect Your character, act in faith, and have pure motives that honor You.

Thank You for this time of waiting, Father. It's difficult to say that, but I know You are working all things for my good. Certainly, I will see the fulfillment of Your promises if I continue to trust in You and do as You instruct. Help me to wait patiently before You until I know Your answer, and please fill me with the courage to pursue Your will with all my heart, mind, soul, and strength. To You be all the glory, honor, and praise in my life and forevermore.

In Jesus's name I pray. Amen.

TO
Worship

Come, let us worship and bow down,
Let us kneel before the LORD our Maker.
—PSALM 95:6

Lord God, how worthy You are of my worship! I rejoice in You and fix my eyes on You. Jesus, You are my Lord, Savior, and Beloved. You are the Almighty One—the One "who is and who was and who is to come" (Revelation 1:8). You are the "Alpha and the Omega, the first and the last, the beginning and the end" (Revelation 22:13). And You are my Advocate. Thank You for being the author and perfecter of my faith. You "sat down at the right hand of the throne of God" (Hebrews 12:2), and You not only direct my path but also give me everything I need along the way. All authority in heaven and on earth has been given to You, Lord Jesus (Matthew 28:18). How grateful I am that You look upon me with love, mercy, and grace.

Jesus, You are the Man of Sorrows. You know the rejection I feel in my heart and have accepted me, becoming the very foundation of my life—You're my salvation, my security, my stability, and my strength. You are my Deliverer and Redeemer—the Lamb of God slain from the foundation of the world. You liberate me from sin and bondage, from the domain of darkness, from my own limitations, and "from the wrath to come" (1 Thessalonians 1:10). You are the Bridegroom—You fill me with joy because of Your love and my eternal union with You. You are the wonderful, priceless, indescribable Gift.

Lord Jesus, You are the Good Shepherd. You have laid down Your "life for the sheep" (John 10:11), made sure we have all we need, comforted us, led us, protected us, and prepared a table before us. We don't deserve how well You care for us. Thank You that no one can snatch us from Your hand; we have eternal life by the blood You shed on the cross. You are also our Great High Priest. You have "passed through the heavens" (Hebrews 4:14) and are seated at the right hand of the throne of grace, making intercession for us and helping us in our time of need.

Jesus, You are the Bread of Life. Whoever comes to You will never go hungry, and whoever believes in You will never thirst. Thank You for filling me up—for providing me with what is good and for delighting me with Your abundance in spirit, soul, body, heart, and mind. You are the beloved Son of God—You have pleased the Father and teach me how to do so as well. You are the Way, the Truth, and the Life. You are the powerful Word of God, who speaks, creates, guides, and fulfills.

You are the Light of the World. Because of Your presence with me through Your indwelling Holy Spirit, I never need to "walk in the darkness, but will have the Light of life" (John 8:12). You are my Comforter and the Mighty One who defends me. You are the One who sets me free from every entanglement and enticement—from everything that hinders the abundant life You have given me. You are my hope, my peace, my Rock, my Refuge, and my Shelter.

You are the head of the church, and all things are under Your feet. You endow Your children with gifts for our mutual edification. You give us every spiritual blessing, purpose, unity, and You lead us in the way we should go. You grant that Your bond servants may "speak Your word with all confidence, while You extend Your hand to heal" (Acts 4:29-30). You empower us to walk in Your will and enable us to be Your ministers of reconciliation.

You are faithful and true—You fulfill all Your promises. You are the Great I Am and Immanuel—"God with us" (Matthew 1:23). You are our trustworthy, merciful, and righteous Judge and the King of Kings, the Lord of Lords, and Sovereign over all. All authority, honor, power, and praise are due Your holy and precious name. You are the Lion of the tribe of Judah—the Root of David. You have "conquered, so that [You] can open the scroll and its seven seals," bringing justice to the world and reclaiming what is rightfully Yours (Revelation 5:5 ESV).

You are the supreme Creator of all that exists. By You "all things were created, both in the heavens and on earth, visible and invisible, whether thrones or dominions or rulers or authorities—all things have been created" through You and for You because You are "before all things, and in [You] all things hold together" (Colossians 1:16–17). You are the victorious One, the risen Messiah, the Resurrection, and the Life. You are our Wonderful Counselor, Mighty God, Everlasting Father, and Prince of Peace.

You are Lord of all! And for this reason, Your name, Jesus, is above all others. And at Your name, precious Savior, one day, every knee will bow, of those who are in heaven and on earth and under the earth, and every tongue will confess that Jesus Christ is Lord, to the glory of God the Father. You alone are worthy of my love, honor, power, allegiance, worship, and adoration now and forevermore! Thank You for making Yourself known to me. May my life bring You praise.

In Jesus's name I pray. Amen.

HOME TO
Heaven

You are my refuge.
Into Your hands I commit my spirit;
deliver me, LORD, my faithful God. . . .
As for me, I trust in the LORD.
—PSALM 31:4–6 NIV

Father, no person knows the day or the hour when You will call them home, but I sense my time is drawing near. I thank You, Jesus, for the great salvation You've given me and the abounding hope I have as the moment I will see You face-to-face approaches. I have no reason to be afraid because I know You have prepared a place for me so I can be with You forever.

But as my time nears, Father, help me say what I need to say to my loved ones. Let no love be left unexpressed, no conflict left unresolved, no forgiveness left ungranted, and no encouragement or gratefulness be left unsaid. Comfort them, Lord Jesus, and may they look to You in their grieving and as they adjust. For those who do not know You as Savior, I pray they would turn to You, confess they need You, and take hold of the redemption You have so freely given. And for my loved ones who profess faith in You, remind them of the hope we have—that we will see each other again and be together for eternity because of Your provision on the cross.

Jesus, into Your hands I commit my spirit with peace and joy. How I long to look upon Your wonderful face and fall at Your feet in worship. Receive me, Lord. Thank You for the life You have given me on this earth. Thank You for the ways You have allowed me to serve You. And thank You for the eternal home You give me in heaven.

In Jesus's name I pray. Amen.

FROM THE **PASTOR'S HEART**
A MONTHLY LETTER FROM DR. CHARLES STANLEY

Dr. Charles Stanley is a much-loved Bible teacher who has spent more than half a century as a caring pastor. Each month, receive his in-depth teaching letter on a topic of faith. You'll be strengthened in doctrine, challenged to grow, and encouraged to stay the course.

FREE
SUBSCRIPTION
PRINT OR
DIGITAL

LET US
pray for you.

Have you experienced the miracle of answered prayer?
We have, and we want to share it. Let us stand with you
in faith, hope, and love, knowing God listens.

CALL US ANYTIME. WE'D BE HONORED TO PRAY FOR YOU.

1-800-789-1473